Rolls-Royce:
The History of The Car

Rolls-Royce:
The History of The Car

MARTIN BENNETT

ARCO PUBLISHING COMPANY, INC. New York

First published 1974

Reprinted 1976, 1978

Published by Arco Publishing Company, Inc.
219 Park Avenue South, New York, N.Y. 10003

Library of Congress Catalog Card Number 74-80995

ISBN 0-668-03619-2

Printed in Great Britain

Contents

List of Illustrations

Foreword

This work was prepared over a period of several years. It would not have been possible without Rolls-Royce Ltd. (Motor Car Division), now Rolls-Royce Motors Ltd., who proved to be a veritable mine of information, photographs, catalogues, brochures and even Owners' Handbooks as supplied with the cars. Their Public Relations Manager, Dennis Miller-Williams spared no trouble in supplying everything I requested, usually from some twelve thousand miles distant. Despite living in Australia I was twice able to undertake research work at the Conduit Street, London, offices of the Company and to take as much material as I needed from the photographic files, and was made most welcome at the Crewe factory where an extremely enjoyable and interesting day was spent.

Jack Barclay Ltd. were also most helpful in supplying photographs of James Young coachwork and showing me around their vast maintenance depot at Battersea. Several superb drawings by Vic Berris and John Ferguson have been reproduced by courtesy of 'Autocar' magazine while the Australian artist John Bull was kind enough to supply a number of his magnificent drawings, many of which were especially prepared for this book. Two of these, depicting beautifully restored veteran *Silver Ghosts*, were reproduced by kind permission of their owners Eric Rainsford and Laurie Vinall by whom the drawings were originally commissioned.

Much of the material on the 'Spirit of Ecstasy' mascot was kindly supplied by Jo Sykes, daughter of Charles Sykes, the mascot's original designer. I am greatly indebted to Mr. Elwood Hansen of California who supplied a complete list of all *Phantom IV* cars with details of their coachwork and original owners. To my knowledge no such list has ever been published before and Rolls-Royce enthusiasts should find it most interesting. Finally I would like to record my thanks to my friends Eric and Betty Cheshire for cooperating with me to take the photographs of their interesting *Silver Cloud* 'Countryman' saloon.

MARTIN I. BENNETT

Acknowledgements

I would like to thank the people listed below for their help in supplying the following photographs and illustration material:

Autocar   97, 121, 210, 237, 257-259

Jack Barclay   98, 99, 100-103, 114, 115, 122, 123, 133, 169, 170, 183-185, 197, 199, 200, 215, 227, 228, 252-255

John Bull   30, 31, 36, 44, 52, 55, 58-62, 71, 72, 75, 76, 80-83, 91, 92, 105-108, 117-119, 135, 136, 139, 157, 161, 191, 194, 231, 232, 264, 265

F. J. Engish   45, 46, 63, 70, 134, 218, 219

David Scott-Moncrieff   129

T. Reich   54, 67, 134, 181

Rolls-Royce Motors Ltd   1-13, 19-29, 33, 34, 39-43, 49, 53, 56, 64, 65, 66, 68, 69, 73, 74, 78, 79, 84-89, 93, 95, 111, 113, 124, 128, 130-132, 140-142, 144-156, 160, 162-167, 171-175, 177-180, 182, 186-190, 192, 195, 198, 208, 209, 211-214, 216, 217, 220-226, 233-236, 238, 240, 242-251, 256, 260-262, 266-278

Jo Sykes   14, 15, 16, 17, 18

Vintage Autos   90, 137

1. The Hon. Charles Stewart Rolls.   2. Sir Frederick Henry Royce, Bart.

Introduction

A great deal of material has already been written on the subject of Rolls-Royce and Bentley motor cars. This book, however, is the only one on the market to cover every model produced by Rolls-Royce Limited and the present Company Rolls-Royce Motors (1971) Limited from the little 10 h.p. of 1904 to the present day *Corniche*. The vast majority of the illustrations in this book have never previously been published. These two facts, I feel, justify the production of this book, which I have attempted to make sufficiently different from other books on the marque to be of interest even to enthusiasts familiar with the excellent works already produced.

No attempt has been made to go into great technical detail in the text, and only the basic facts as I know them have been dealt with; this is therefore a predominantly pictorial book. Each model is illustrated as profusely as possible and a few illustrations of a technical nature have been included.

Rolls-Royce and Bentley cars are regarded by most people as the world's finest. However, most also regard these cars as reserved only for the very rich. This is unfortunate as many people who can, without knowing it, afford to own the world's best are content to motor in modern automotive bread and butter, which is the latest and greatest this year and obsolete next year. Shortly before this introduction was written an acquaintance of mine changed his modern, expensive car for a rather nice 1951 Mk. VI Bentley which he promptly brought around to show me. While we were taking it for a run he remarked that for the money he paid for this car the majority of people would have bought a "sardine can". The comparatively high petrol consumption of such cars is more than offset by the lack of depreciation, which is surely the greatest single factor in the cost of owning a car. In fact all pre-war models and some post-war models are actually appreciating in value quite steadily. In these days of galloping inflation an elderly Rolls-Royce or Bentley is a safe investment. The person who buys a new or nearly new mass-produced car every year or two pays for the best but never attains it. The joys of Rolls-Royce motoring are not the prerogative of the wealthy owner of the *Shadows* and *Clouds* of recent years.

3.

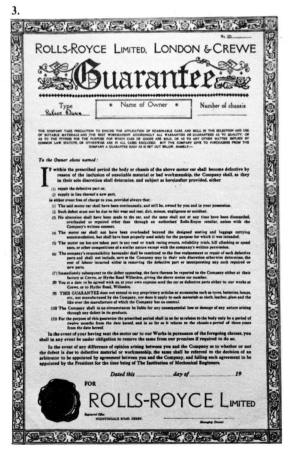

4. *Above* the present-day factory at Crewe.
5. *Below* Early Rolls-Royce Motor Cars in Cooke Street Factory.

Long Established
Principles and Traditions

When Rolls-Royce devise or refine an idea, it will normally be found that they are reluctant to drop the idea in favour of a more modern system hardly capable of doing the job in any superior fashion to the original or old-fashioned system. The Rolls-Royce braking system immediately springs to mind. When disc brakes had become fashionable Rolls-Royce were criticised because they insisted on clinging to the "old-fashioned" drums (on all four wheels) with an equally old-fashioned servo unit originally manufactured under Hispano-Suiza patents. However, the Company promised to make the change to a more modern system when it became as smooth, progressive, fade-free and above all, as quiet, as the existing system. The appropriate changes were made for the *Silver Shadow* and Bentley *T* series, announced in October, 1965.

From 1933 the *Phantom II* was fitted with an admirable Rolls-Royce refinement which also stayed to grace every Rolls-Royce and Bentley car until all-independent suspension was introduced for the *Silver Shadow*. This was the ride control which took the form of hydraulic shock absorbers, the loading of which was automatically adjusted by an hydraulic governing device to suit the road speed of the car. A lever was provided on the steering column by which means the driver could vary the riding of the car, to suit rough or indifferent road surfaces, independently of the governor. At first the system operated on all four dampers but in its post-war form only the rear dampers were affected and the governor was deleted, the adjustment being left to the will of the driver.

A novel and interesting feature of the Rolls-Royce 40/50 h.p. models from 1906 until 1933 and of the pre-*Silver Ghost* models, was the throttle governor which maintained the road speed of the car according to the setting of the lever mounted on the steering column. When encountering a hill the throttle was automatically opened the required degree and shut again on down-grades. The governor could, of course, be over-ridden by the driver by means of the accelerator pedal.

The Rolls-Royce torsional crankshaft vibration damper was an invention of Royce aimed at curing the torsional crankshaft vibrations to which his 30 h.p. six-cylinder model of 1905 was particularly prone. This device, which became known as the Slipper Flywheel, took the form of a friction-disc clutch and flywheel mounted at the forward end of the crankshaft and became an integral feature of every Rolls-Royce motor car engine from 1911 to the present day.

The same principle was discovered by another great engineer of the period, Dr Frederick Lanchester, who promptly patented his invention, but as no royalties were paid to Lanchesters by Rolls-Royce it may be assumed that some agreement was reached between

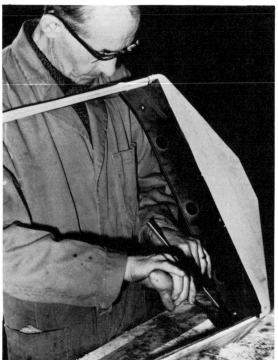

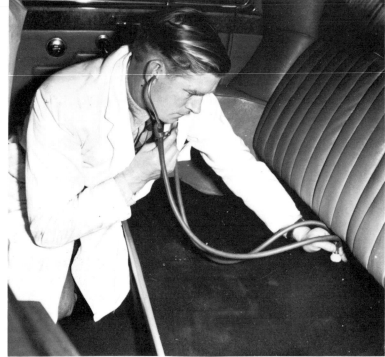

6. *Above left* a craftsman hand-soldering a stainless steel radiator shell.

7. *Above right* Yes, at Rolls-Royce they really do listen for back axle whine with stethoscopes.

the two companies.

It is well-tried principles such as these that prompt people to remark that Rolls-Royces are steeped in tradition. The Rolls-Royce tradition, however, lies in the fact that the cars are built today to the same exacting standards originally set by Sir Henry Royce and maintained after his death by his successors, including Mr Harry Grylls, the Motor Car Division's Chief Engineer from 1951 until 1969. The pride which Rolls-Royce employees take in their work is an important tradition largely responsible for the Rolls-Royce retention of the title 'Best Car in the World'. As the brochure on the Rolls-Royce *Silver Shadow* and Bentley *T* series cars states: *The tradition of meticulous attention to even the smallest detail, both in the design and workmanship of Rolls-Royce and Bentley cars is followed as closely today as it was in the days of Sir Henry Royce.* The classic Rolls-Royce radiator, has, in one form or another, been a feature of every Rolls-Royce car ever made, with the exception of the ill-fated, bonnetless town-carriage of 1905 (known as the *Invisible Engine* model), of which only two were built. Royce himself always expressed the opinion that the famous sharp-edged structure was impractical and unnecessarily costly to make, (specialised craftsmen must be employed full-time on that job to this very day, hand-soldering stainless steel sheets). However, Claude Johnson, the Company's General Manager, ruled that the radiator was far too much of a distinctive feature to be recklessly abandoned.

Rolls-Royce never object to employing other manufacturers' ideas where these prove satisfactory for their needs. Perhaps the most obvious example of this, together with the automatic gearbox, is the classic Rolls-Royce braking system. This was adopted by the Company in 1925 and retained until 1965 when a change was made to a more modern system. This ingenious device comprised a friction

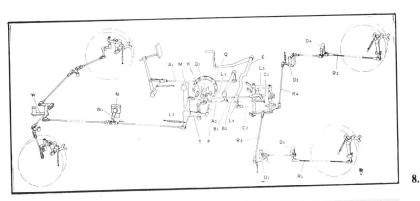

8. Pre-war braking system showing servo linkage.

9 Rolls-Royce brake servo unit.

clutch driven by the transmission and a system of rods. Hydraulic circuits were also incorporated at a later date. A fixed percentage of the effort exerted by the driver in the brake pedal was diverted to the friction clutch, which harnessed the car's own inertia for braking power. An admirably simple and highly effective system. In their final form the combination of Rolls-Royce servo and drum brakes proved extremely powerful and free from fade and snatch. A Rolls-Royce *Silver Cloud III* road tested by *Motor* magazine exhibited traces of fade but was still, however, appreciably superior to a car equipped with discs. Later Rolls-Royce claimed (and *Motor* confirmed) that the brakes of the test car were maladjusted, thus accounting for the slight fade. It is therefore reasonable to assume that if faulty Rolls-Royce brakes proved superior to discs then correctly-adjusted brakes would show a more obvious superiority. One wonders why and how the Company allowed an incorrectly-adjusted vehicle to pass for road-testing in a reputable journal.

To simplify the task of lubrication, Rolls-Royce once fitted their cars with a completely centralised chassis lubrication system supplying oil from a reservoir, and operated by a foot-pedal. The system first appeared in its basic form (partially centralised) in 1929 on the *Twenty* and featured on all models from 1932 until 1959 in a completely centralised form.

In 1959 when the Rolls-Royce *Silver Cloud II* and Bentley *S2* series were introduced the 'one-shot' was abandoned in favour of

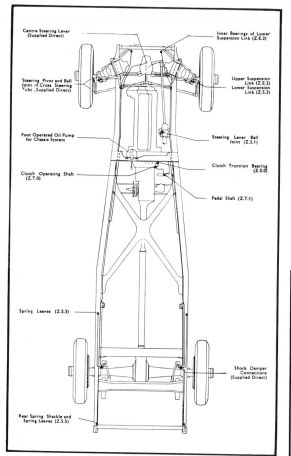

grease points (twenty-one, for attention every 12,000 miles). It would seem that the Company noticed that cars in for maintenance showed evidence of negligence as regards chassis lubrication and one must draw the unhappy but logical conclusion that some owners were too lazy or forgetful to depress the pedal periodically. Occasionally, the system was known to have broken-down, through no fault of the owner, and parts starved of oil owing to blockage were subjected to rapid wear.

Rolls-Royce owe the design of their independent front suspension introduced in 1935 to the General Motors Corporation. The choice followed years of investigation into the various systems of i.f.s. available at the time and, although none was up to Rolls-Royce standards, the General Motors system proved most suitable. A ride in an i.f.s.-equipped Rolls-Royce, in excess of 40 m.p.h. over the most brutal roads will demonstrate that, as refined by Rolls-Royce, the borrowed suspension design is beyond reproach.

10. *Above* A plan showing points lubricated by centralised system.
11. *Below* The oil reservoir mounted on the bulkhead.

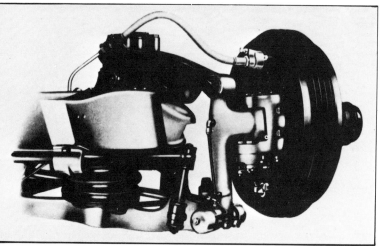

12. *Above* Post-war independent front suspension layout.
13. *Below* Close-up and exploded diagram of the drip-plug found in the centralised lubrication system.

The Spirit of Ecstasy

Spirit of Ecstasy has selected road travel as her supreme delight and has alighted on the prow of a Rolls-Royce car to revel in the freshness of the air and the musical sound of her fluttering draperies. These are the words of the celebrated artist Charles Sykes in describing his fairy-like creation *Spirit of Ecstasy* or *Flying Lady* as she has become erroneously but more commonly known.

This lovely piece of sculpture, now so well-known among lovers of fine motor-cars, originally appeared on the Barker-bodied *Silver Ghost* tourer of Lord Montagu of Beaulieu, the man who initiated her creation at a time when the most tasteless of mascots were to be seen perched upon the radiators of all too many British cars.

Most Rolls-Royce enthusiasts are of the impression that the model for the original *Spirit of Ecstasy* was Lord Montagu's private secretary, Eleanor Thornton, and according to the present Lord Montagu *this figure may have been, and probably was, a composite derived from the various models who sat for Sykes,* though he goes on to say that *the features are unmistakably those of Eleanor Thornton.* However, Jo Sykes, Charles' daughter, dismisses this as legend and says Miss Thornton was *of a rather statuesque build quite unlike that of the fairy-like figure* that has become as much an instantly recognised feature of Rolls-Royce cars as the Grecian radiator and entwined R's of the monogram.

Miss Thornton was a great friend of Sykes and his wife Jessica, and their daughter Jo remembers her well. She did indeed pose for many of Sykes' bronzes, notably the *Bacchante*, *Phryne*, the woman in the group called *The Arcadians* and other works. These were exhibited in the Royal Academy Summer Exhibitions and the Salon de Paris in the years 1910, 1911 and 1912.

An agreement was drawn up between the Company and Charles Sykes in 1911 and in that year the Company announced that *arrangements are being made by which an owner of a Rolls-Royce may acquire one of these figureheads for a few pounds.* The copyright of the *Spirit of Ecstasy* was owned by Rolls-Royce under this agreement, and Charles Sykes was to be the sole maker of the mascots for as long as he was able. In 1920 the Company entered the *Spirit of Ecstasy* in the 'Concours Mondiale des Bouchons d'Automobiles' organised by the magazine *L'Auto*.

Charles Sykes was presented with the gold medal much to his great surprise and joy as he had no idea that the Company had entered his pet creation. In the following year *Spirit of Ecstasy* became standard equipment on all Rolls-Royce cars and has remained so ever since.

In 1928 Jo, Charles Sykes' daughter, (also an artist and sculptor) took over the finishing of the individual mascots and conducted the

14. The Spirit of Ecstasy' in miniature form, mounted with wine cup for presentation.

15. The original 'Spirit of Ecstasy' for the 40/50 h.p. cars.
16. The second mascot introduced for the 20/25 h.p. models.

business side in order to release her father for other pressing commissioned works, but the same care in production was always maintained, father and daughter often working together on rush orders.

In the winter of 1915, Lord Montagu, who was then Inspector of Mechanical Transport in India, was returning to his post after a difficult conference in London. Miss Thornton sailed with him on the *S.S. Persia.* On December 30th the vessel was torpedoed and sunk off Crete. Miss Thornton was drowned but Lord Montagu was picked up by the steamer *Nung Chow,* along with ten other survivors after having spent four days in an open life-boat. He returned to England and was able to read his own obituaries.

According to the present Lord Montagu, his father *seldom referred to that tragic incident at sea in later life, though to friends he would occasionally murmur sadly,* Poor Thorn. It was terrible. *But perhaps the memorial that Eleanor Thornton would have appreciated most is the statuette on the radiator of every Rolls-Royce car ever since. It is a fitting tribute to a girl who brought efficiency into my father's professional life and serenity into his private life; and she handled an equivocal situation with dignity.*

Jo Sykes remembers how through the years Thorn was spoken of with affection and admiration.

17. The Kneeling Lady. She was devised for the more streamlined *Phantom III* in 1935.

The Bentley Cars

In the 'twenties the name Bentley was perhaps the most well-known and respected in the high-speed sporting car class. At first, under the administration of W.O. Bentley, these cars were built strictly for their performance—high noise level and hard springs ruling out their use as luxury carriages. Tremendous success in Le Mans twenty-four hour races put Bentleys at the forefront in racing, and a 3-litre or 4½-litre Bentley, its Van Den Plas coachwork resplendent in the British Racing Green livery in which these cars are most familiar, is still far from being a rare sight on British roads today.

In 1929, Bentley Motors introduced an 8-litre chassis intended for the luxury carriage market. These cars, of which about a hundred were built, were developed from the 6½-litre and marked the end of the company as a separate entity. The Depression of 1929 killed Bentley Motors financially, and W.O. Bentley sold out to Rolls-Royce Limited following an unsuccessful bid by the Napier Company.

18. The *Bentley* winged-B mascot as used in the early Rolls-Royce built *Bentleys*.

The Royce
and
Early Rolls-Royce Cars

The story of how Henry Royce purchased a second-hand Decauville and decided he could build a superior car has been told and re-told so many times that I will not relate it again. We need only deal here with the actual cars rather than with the already well-known story behind their creation.

The first 10 h.p. Royce car was driven out of the Cooke Street, Manchester works of Royce Ltd, by Royce himself on 1 April 1904. The engine of this little creation had two cylinders of $3\frac{3}{4}$ inch bore and 5 inch stroke and was said to have developed 12 b.h.p. at 1,000 r.p.m. The valve layout was overhead inlet and side exhaust, a layout that appeared again forty-two years later with the introduction of the *Mk. VI* Bentley. The drive from the engine was transmitted to the three-speed gearbox through a leather-lined cone-type clutch and universal joint. The foot-brake operated on the drive-shaft. The degree of silence and smoothness achieved by Royce set the standard for the cars bearing the name 'Rolls-Royce', which quickly became recognised as the world's best.

The second Royce car became the property of A.E. Claremont, Royce's partner in the F.H. Royce & Co. Electrical Engineering venture. Claremont was also a director of the Trafford Park Power & Light Co. and of W.T. Glover & Co. Ltd, and it was Henry Edmunds of Glovers who became the owner of the third Royce car. It was Edmunds who first arranged for Royce and the Hon. C.S. Rolls to meet.

After Rolls had agreed to sell all that Royce could produce, the 10 h.p. remained in production under the magic name of Rolls-Royce. These charming little cars carried a distinctively-shaped radiator, which in one form or another, has graced every Rolls-Royce car right up to the *Corniche* of 1971. At first the badge on the radiator was oval-shaped and inscribed with the name Rolls-Royce. Later, the famous rectangular monogram was evolved.

One Royce car was still in use by the Company up until 1923 when it was destroyed. The destruction of this car may be compared to the senseless destruction by George Jackson Churchward of the historic Great Western Railway broad gauge locomotives *Lord of the Isles* and *North Star* because they occupied *valuable workshop space*. In each case no thought was given to future generations of enthusiasts. It is not easily forgivable that the last remaining Royce car was not preserved for posterity. It also seems rather sad that the car should be destroyed after a life of a mere nineteen years.

By grouping three separate 4 inch by 5 inch cylinders a 3,000 c.c. 15 h.p. car was evolved. Royce more logically developed two further models, a four-cylinder 20 h.p. and a six-cylinder 30 h.p., by grouping pairs of cylinders as used for the 10 h.p. and in so doing was able to

19. 1905 10 h.p. 2-cylinder Rolls-Royce. The radiator is recognisably Rolls-Royce though the badge is the early oval type. This car is exhibited in the Kensington Science Museum, London.

20. One of Royce's first three 10 h.p. cars. This is believed to be the last of the three destroyed by the Company in 1923.

21. 1905 10 h.p. 2-cylinder Rolls-Royce. This car was originally owned by a doctor who drove over 100,000 miles in it between 1905 and 1920. It is now owned by Rolls-Royce Motors (1971) Ltd. Chassis No. 20163.

22. 1905 15 h.p. 3-cylinder Rolls-Royce. The example shown is at the Derby factory probably towards the end of its working life.
23. A 20 h.p. 4-cylinder Rolls-Royce. The chassis shown was restored by Stanley Sears.

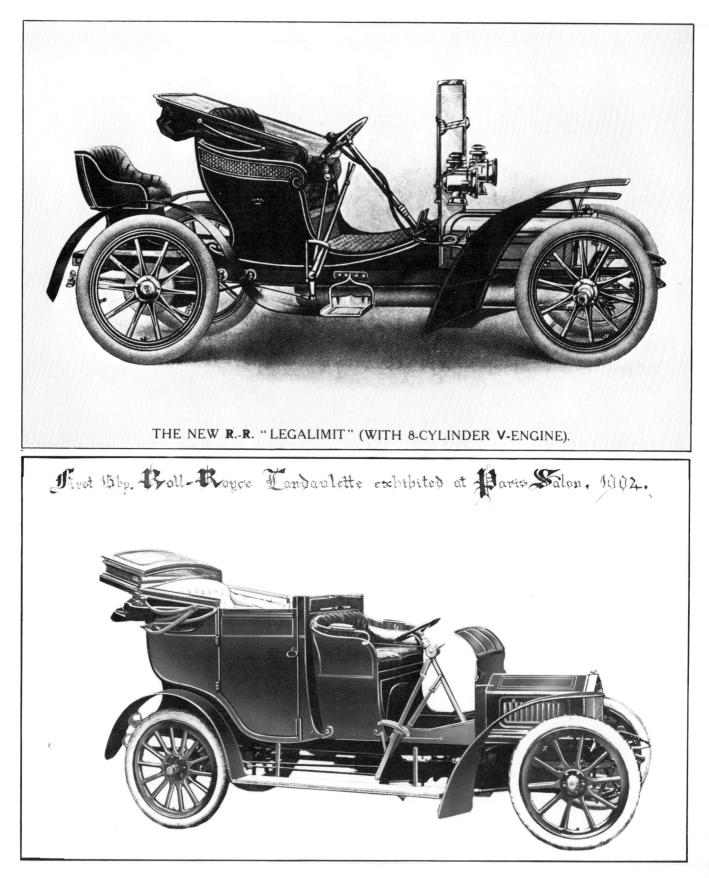

THE NEW **R.-R.** "LEGALIMIT" (WITH 8-CYLINDER **V**-ENGINE).

First 15hp. Roll-Royce Landaulette exhibited at Paris Salon, 1904.

standardise many of the main engine parts.

A fifth, much more interesting, engine was introduced for use in the 'bonnetless' town carriages and *Legalimits*; the latter name derived from the fact that the car was so low-geared as to render it incapable of exceeding the then ruling speed limit of 20 m.p.h. This was the 3,500 c.c. V-8, one of the very first V-8's and obviously wasted on such ponderous machines as those for which it was designed. The eight cylinders were arranged in a ninety-degree vee and although it would have been conceivable to use the standard cylinder blocks as used in the two-, four- and six-cylinder engines this was not done and new blocks were designed with vertical valves; that is to say, the valves were arranged at 45 degrees from the cylinders. Bore and stroke were the same at $3\frac{1}{4}$ inches. Only two of the invisible engine or bonnetless cars were completed and, mercifully, only one *Legalimit*. The one-model policy of 1907 unfortunately spelt the doom of the V-8, otherwise it would have been interesting to have seen what Royce could have done with such an advanced engine.

Backed by the sporting enthusiasm of C.S. Rolls, Rolls-Royce quickly made a name for themselves in motor racing, with Percy Northey's *Light Twenty* Rolls-Royce taking second place in the 1905 Tourist Trophy race on the Isle of Man. Two *Light Twenties* were entered in this race but the second one suffered a smashed gearbox less than a mile from the start at the hands of C.S.R. himself. However, in the following years T.T. Rolls was able to redeem himself and the name of Rolls-Royce by bringing his car over the finishing line in first place at an average speed of 39.3 m.p.h.

So it was that Rolls-Royce had a range of very successful designs at their disposal and it must seem strange to some that the entire range, from the little 10 h.p. to the powerful six-cylinder 30 h.p. was abandoned. Indeed it does seem strange until one considers the very magnificence of the 40/50 h.p. model upon which the Company's 'one-model policy' of 1909 was based.

26. Early patter steering-wheel with throttle governor and ignition timing controls.

PRE-SILVER GHOST MODELS.

Model	Year Bore	Stroke	c.c.	h.p.	Clutch	Gearbox	Final Drive	Suspension	Brakes	Wheelbase	Track	Number Made	Chassis Price
2-cylinder	1904-1905 1905 3¾"	5"	1,800	10	Leather-lined cone type.	Three-speed.	Fully-floating live axle. Spur-type gears.	Semi-elliptic.	Transmission foot-brake. Handbrake operates on rear wheels.	6'3"	4'0"	3 Royce 16 Rolls-Royce.	£395
3-cylinder	1906 3-15/16" 1905 4"	5" 5"	2,000 3,000	15	Leather-lined cone type.	Three-speed.	Fully-floating live axle. Spur-type gears.	Semi-elliptic.	Transmission foot-brake. Handbrake operates on rear wheels.	8'7"		6	£500
4-cylinder	1905 4" 1905 3¾"	5" 5"	4,000 3,600	20	Leather-lined cone type.	Light model four-speed (overdrive fourth). Heavy model three-speed. Light model four-speed.	Platform rear.	Semi-elliptic front. Platform rear.	Transmission foot-brake. Handbrake operates on rear wheels.	Light model 8'10". Heavy model 9'6".	Light model 4'4". Heavy model 4'8".	40	£650
6-cylinder	1905-1906 4"	5"	6,000	30	Leather-lined cone type. (overdrive fourth)	Four-speed (overdrive fourth).	Platform rear.	Semi-elliptic front. Platform rear.	Transmission foot-brake. Handbrake operates on rear wheels.	Short Wheelbase 9'8½" Long wheelbase 9'10"	4'8"	37	£890
'Legalimit' and Bonnetless V-8's	1905-1906 3¾"	3¾"	3,500		Leather-lined cone type.	Three-speed.		Semi-elliptic.	Transmission foot-brake. Handbrake operates on rear wheels.	Bonnetless 7'6" "Legalimit" 8'10"	4'4"	2 Bonnetless cars. 1 Legalimit	

The Silver Ghost

Late in 1906 the 40/50 h.p. model was introduced to the world at the London Motor show. The first 40/50 h.p. chassis was displayed alongside a 30 h.p. Barker limousine on the stand of C.S. Rolls and Company. This new model was destined to make a more profound impression on the motoring world than any other car in history. The *Silver Ghost*, as it became known, swiftly established itself as the ultimate in luxury motoring; truly 'The Best Car in the World.'

The 40/50 h.p. differed from the 30 h.p. chiefly in its size and in its engine, a side-valve unit of 4½ inch bore and stroke with its cylinders cast in two blocks of three rather than in three blocks of two.

The thirteenth 40/50 h.p. chassis to be completed (chassis No. 60551) was selected by Johnson and fitted with a handsome touring body by Barker. The aluminium paint and silver-plated lamps and fittings of this car earned it the name *Silver Ghost,* which the car still carries engraved on a plate attached to the dashboard. *Silver Ghost* became a demonstration car and was put to the test in a 2,000 mile trial under the supervision of the Royal Automobile Club. During this trial a figure of better than 20 m.p.g. was achieved on the road between London and Glasgow, a truly magnificent achievement for so large a car with an engine capacity of 7,036 c.c. Following this effort, the car was entered in the Scottish Reliability Trial. After 629 miles an involuntary stop was caused by a petrol tap shaking shut, but after this brief halt, and after the trial, *Silver Ghost* continued to run day and night, resting only on Sundays, until 15,000 miles had been covered. 14,371 miles had therefore been covered without an involuntary stop—a world record. The cost of parts required to put the car back into new condition was £2-2s-7d.

27. The original *Silver Ghost*. The coachwork for this car, now owned by Rolls-Royce was by Barker.

28. The Cat and Fiddle', where a commemorative meeting of *Silver Ghosts* was held. AX 201, the Company's original *Silver Ghost* can be seen on the left.

29. Controls of AX201, the Company's original *Silver Ghost*. Note controls on the steering wheel for the Throttle Governor ('Fast', 'Slow') and ignition ('Early', 'Late').

In July 1908 a new Rolls-Royce factory at Derby was opened by Lord Montagu of Beaulieu. Production at Derby was concentrated on the 40/50 h.p., all other models being discontinued. This 'one-model' policy was instigated by Claude Johnson who saw no future in building five different models. Various modified versions of the *Silver Ghost* were tried: the first of these was not released to the public because Royce considered the four modified cars too noisy. The power output of these four cars was increased to 70 h.p. by raising the compression ratio and reverting to the overhead inlet side exhaust valve arrangement. Two of the experimental cars, named

White Knave and *Silver Rogue* were in the International Touring Car Trial in 1908 with *Silver Rogue* winning in its class. The following year the stroke of the *Silver Ghost* was increased to $4\frac{3}{4}$ inches, giving a capacity of 7,428 c.c. In the same year, the four-speed overdrive gearbox was changed to a three-speed.

30. The 1910 *Silver Ghost* Tulip-seat touring car, is owned, and was restored by Laurie Vinall of Brighton, South Australia. Chassis No. 1388.

31. A 1912 Rolls-Royce *Silver Ghost* touring car. It is owned and was restored by Eric Rainsford of Springfield, South Australia. Chassis No. 1853E.

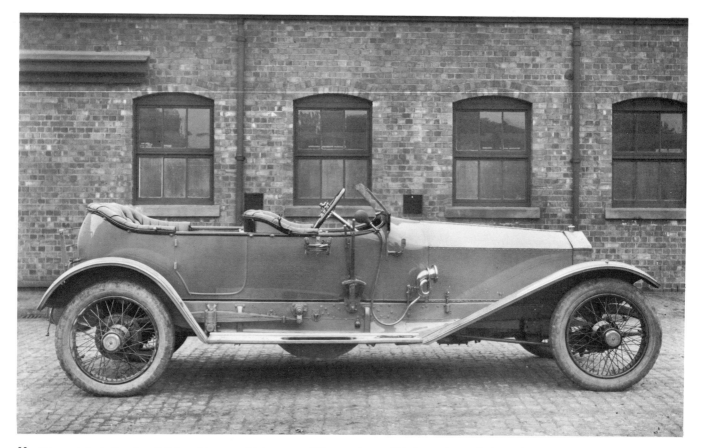

32. The original 'London-Edinburgh' car, which in 1911 was driven from London to Edinburgh and back entirely on top gear, and afterwards without alteration, was driven on Brooklands at 78.36 m.p.h. The design of the body, a singularly attractive one for the period was reproduced, with modifications for many years afterwards.

The next modified version of the Ghost was the London—Edinburgh model introduced to the public in 1911. This model originated when a *Silver Ghost* chassis was equipped with underslung cantilever rear springs, raised compression ratio and larger carburettor for a special trial run between London and Edinburgh using top gear only. Most London—Edinburgh chassis were fitted with narrow sporting tourer bodies similar to the one fitted to the prototype (chassis 1701E). The London—Edinburgh trial resulted in the car achieving a fuel consumption figure of a remarkable 24.32 miles per gallon and later, without alteration or adjustment, a speed of 78.26 miles per hour at Brooklands. Also in 1911, an almost standard London—Edinburgh chassis fitted with streamlined racing body and capable of running at a walking pace in top gear, attained a speed of 101.8 m.p.h. on the Brooklands track. Today the London—Edinburgh *Silver Ghost* is perhaps the most sought-after of all Rolls-Royce models, commanding prices in the £10,000 and upwards range.

In 1913 four *Silver Ghosts* were entered in the Austrian Alpine Trials, the result being that Rolls-Royce took prizes for 1st place, 3rd place, fastest lap, fastest final lap, and best all-round performance; a truly remarkable feat. As a result of the Alpine Trials a reversion was made to a four-speed gearbox, with direct drive on fourth speed. A new sporting version, with increases in the height of the radiator and ground clearance, was introduced and named the 'Continental' model. These cars quickly became known as *Alpine Eagles* as a fitting tribute to the wonderful results achieved by Rolls-Royce cars in the Alpine Trials.

33. 1914 Rolls-Royce *Silver Ghost.* 'Alpine Eagle' Tourer.
34. WHP 32. One of the team which triumphed with over-whelming success in the 1913 Austrian Alpine Contest.

35. 1922 *Silver Ghost* Tourer by H. J. Mulliner, registration No. 33KG. This photograph was taken in 1945 when the car was used by H.R.H. The Duke of Gloucester, then Governor-General of Australia. It is now owned by Mr Anthony James of Victoria, Australia and bears the Registered No. RR257.

During the Great War Rolls-Royce *Silver Ghosts* performed valiantly as ambulances, staff-cars and, as any reader of T.E. Lawrence's *Seven Pillars of Wisdom* will know, as armoured cars. These remarkable machines covered many thousands of miles in the desert and even though they were burdened with incredibly heavy armoured bodies showed themselves capable of speeds in excess of 50 m.p.h. and were almost completely immune to mechanical breakdowns.

After the war the Ghost was put back into production with electric starting and lighting. Almost the entire electrical system was designed and manufactured by Rolls-Royce. Various other improvements were made, including, at the end of 1923, four-wheel brakes with the famous mechanical servo.

Derby ceased producing the *Silver Ghost* in 1925 but production continued for a year or so at Springfield, Massachusetts, where Claude Johnson had opened a new factory in 1919. During this remarkable production run of nearly twenty years 7,876 chassis were produced and the price for the chassis only, almost doubled from £980 in 1907 to £1,850 in 1923.

THE 40/50 h.p. 'SILVER GHOST'
IN PRODUCTION 1906–1925
SPRINGFIELD MODEL 1921–1926

'1924 Rolls-Royce Silver Ghost Open Tourer by Barker'   36.

ENGINE
Six cylinders in two blocks of three. *1906* 4½ inch bore by 4½ inch stroke giving 7,036 c.c. *1909* 4½ inch bore by 4¾ inch stroke giving 7,428 c.c. Side valves operated from single camshaft through exposed tappets. 7-bearing crankshaft. *1911* 'Slipper Flywheel' vibration damper. Twin-jet carburettor with governor to maintain road speed set by hand lever on steering column quadrant. Electric starting from 1919 onwards. *1921* Starting carburettor, twin ignition system.

CLUTCH
Cone type, leather lined.

GEARBOX
1906 Four speeds with overdrive fourth.
1909 Three speeds.
1913 Four speeds, direct drive fourth.

PROPELLER SHAFT
1906 Open shaft and radius rods.
1911 Torque tube.

STEERING
Worm and nut type.

SUSPENSION
1906 Semi-elliptic front, platform rear.
1908 Semi-elliptic front and rear, friction shock absorbers.
1911 London—Edinburgh cars, cantilever rear springs.
1912 Standard model cantilevers.

BRAKES
1906 Transmission footbrake, rear drums for handbrake.
1913 Footbrake with rear drums.
1924 Four-wheel brakes, servo assisted.

ELECTRICAL SYSTEM
1906 Bosch or 1913 Watford magneto plus battery ignition.
1914 C.A.V. lighting system available.
1919 Electric lighting system standard.

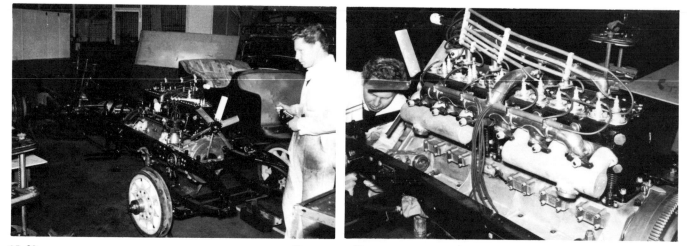

37. 38. Two views of a Veteran *Silver Ghost* under restoration at the Battersea premises of Jack Barclay Ltd.

PRINCIPAL DIMENSIONS

Overall length	*1906*	15′ 0″ short chassis, 15′ 7¼″ long chassis.
	1914	15′ 10¼″
	1923	16′ 4¾″ long chassis.
Wheelbase	*1906*	11′ 3½″ short chassis, 11′ 11½″ long chassis.
	1914	11′ 11½″
	1923	12′ 0″ short chassis, 12′ 6½″ long chassis.
Track		4′ 8″

NUMBER PRODUCED

6,173 plus 1,703 Springfield models.

CHASSIS NUMBERS

60359-92	1907	PP, LW	1919
60700-99	1907-8	TW, CW, FW, BW,	
919-1015	1908-9	AE, EE, RE, PE,	
1100-2699	1909-13	YE, UE, LE, GE, TE	1920

From mid-1913 onwards each chassis number had a suffix of two letters, as follows:

		CE, NE, AG, LG, MG,	
		JG, UG	1921
		UG, SG, TG, KG, PG,	
CA, NA	1913-14	RG, YG, ZG, HG	1922
MA, AB, EB, RB, PB,		LK, NK, PK	1923
YB, UB, LB, GB, TB	1914	EM, LM, RM, TM,	
TB, BD, AD, ED, RD	1915	AU	1924
RD, CB, PD, AC	1916-17	EU	1925

Certain of these chassis numbers were issued twice, the second car having an 'E' suffix, e.g. 1826E.

Some numbers from these series were issued to Springfield chassis. In most series the number 13 was not used.

The New Phantom

By the twenties the *Silver Ghost* model was becoming more than a little old-fashioned, and although the *New Phantom*, or *Phantom I* as it became known, was much faster both in acceleration and top speed, the more old-fashioned *Ghost* features were retained, including the clumsy notched gear-gate. In fact, apart from its new engine and plate-type clutch, the *Phantom* had little to distinguish it from the *Ghost* and it would seem that it had only been introduced as a temporary measure while the *Phantom II* was being prepared.

The *Phantom* engine was a pushrod-operated overhead valve affair like that of the *Twenty*. The bore and stroke were $4\frac{1}{4}$ inches and $5\frac{1}{2}$ inches as compared to the $4\frac{1}{2}$ inches and $4\frac{3}{4}$ inches of the *Ghost*. The result of these dimensional changes was an increase in the cubic capacity to 7,668 c.c. and a decrease in treasury horsepower to 43.3 h.p. Although the *Phantom* was thus more powerful than the *Ghost* it was cheaper to tax because the rated horsepower was lower by some five horsepower, and at £1 per horsepower this was no small saving in 1925. The chief difference between the *Phantom* engine and that of the *Twenty* was that the former had two blocks of three cylinders, like the *Ghost*, whereas the latter's cylinder block was a single casting.

From 1926 until as late as 1931 the American version of the *Phantom I* was produced at the Springfield, Massachusetts factory. This differed from the British version in many ways, including the provision of left-hand steering and a central gear lever.

39. *Phantom I* Saloon by H.J. Mulliner.

40. Rolls-Royce *Phantom I* Cabriolet-de-Ville, by Hooper.

41. 1927 *Phantom I* Brougham by Clarke of Wolverhampton. This is the famous car with Louis XIV furnishings which later passed into the Sears collection. Since this photograph was taken a 'basketwork' finish has been applied to the lower panels of the rear compartment. Chassis No. 76TC.

Although the *Phantom I* has never been the collectors' item that the *Ghost* is, the price commanded today by really first-class cars, even replica-bodied examples, suggests that the model is much more popular than previously. I know of a *Phantom I* in Australia that has been driven as everyday transport by one owner for the last thirty-five years, often being called upon to travel at very high speeds over considerable distances.

42. *Phantom I* Limousine by Park Ward.
43. *Phantom I* with typical touring coachwork.

44. 45. 46. The 1925 *Phantom I* shown in these three views is owned by Mr Don Sheil of Melbourne, Australia. The superbly rakish boat-tail coachwork was built in Melbourne on the magnificently restored chassis No. 11RC.

THE PHANTOM I
IN PRODUCTION 1925–1929

ENGINE

Six cylinders in two blocks of three, $4\frac{1}{4}$ inch bore by $5\frac{1}{2}$ inch stroke giving 7,668 c.c. and rated by the R.A.C. at 43.3 h.p. Overhead valves in cast iron head. *1928* aluminium head. Seven bearing crankshaft with 'Slipper drive', twin-jet carburettor and starting carburettor, centrifugal governor. Battery and magneto ignition systems. Electric starter.

CLUTCH

Single dry plate type.

GEARBOX

Four speeds.

PROPELLER SHAFT

Torque tube.

FINAL DRIVE

Fully floating rear axle with spiral bevel final drive.

STEERING

Worm and nut.

SUSPENSION

1925 Semi-elliptic front, cantilever rear, adjustable friction shock absorbers.

1926 Front hydraulic shock absorbers.

1927 Hydraulic shock absorbers all round.

BRAKES

Four-wheel system, servo-assisted.

PRINCIPAL DIMENSIONS

Overall length: 15' $10\frac{1}{4}$" short chassis; 16' $4\frac{3}{4}$" long chassis.

Wheelbase: 11' $11\frac{1}{4}$" short chassis; 12' $6\frac{1}{2}$" long chassis.

Track: Short chassis: 4' 9" front, 4' 8" rear.

Long chassis: 4' $10\frac{1}{2}$" front, 4' $9\frac{1}{2}$" rear.

NUMBER PRODUCED

2,212 plus 1,241 Springfield models

CHASSIS SERIES (DERBY CHASSIS)

MC, RC, HC, LC, SC	1925-6
DC, TC, YC, NC	1926
EF, LF, RF, UF	1927
EH, FH, AL, WR	1928
CL, WR, KR	1928-9
OR	1929
Total 2,212	

The Phantom 11

In 1929 the *New Phantom,* as it was then known, gave way to the *Phantom II.* Without any increase in price, the Phantom had been radically redesigned resulting in a very fine car having little in common with its noble but somewhat old-fashioned predecessor other than the cylinder bore and stroke dimensions. In fact, the *Phantom II* had more in common with the successful 20 h.p., being virtually an enlarged edition of that car. The most notable change was in the suspension which now comprised semi-elliptics front and rear, the rear ones being underslung. Like the *Twenty,* the engine, clutch and gearbox were in one unit. The engine itself was fundamentally redesigned, although the bore and stroke remained unchanged, with a new cross-flow head (still in aluminium) and self-cleaning oil filter which was scraped clean by a mechanism connected to the clutch linkage. At first the carburettor fitted was similar to that of the *Phantom I* but in 1933 a new single jet semi-expanding type was introduced together with a large cylindrical air-silencer and filter. A starting carburettor was provided, which on later models was linked to the extra oil control. The carburettor was still of Rolls-Royce manufacture as was most of the electrical system. The *Phantom II* saw the introduction of the centralised chassis lubrication system. At first this was somewhat complex, having separate systems for the frame, front axle and rear axle, but from 1933 flexible pipes were used to obviate this complication. This arrangement considerably lightened the work of the mechanic or chauffeur who had to lubricate no fewer than eighty-four points on a *Phantom I* every thousand miles.

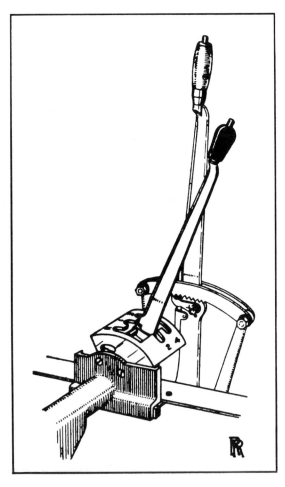

Not only was the *Phantom II* remarkably fast for its size but it possessed a certain grace of proportion not hitherto seen on a Rolls-Royce and, indeed, not seen since. This was achieved by a reduction in the height of the car resulting from underslung rear springs, the extremely long, tapered bonnet and the fact that the steering wheel was almost exactly half way between the axles.

As introduced, the *Phantom II* was an exceptionally good car, but of course Royce and the Company were not satisfied. Between 1929 and 1935 more than sixty changes were made to the specification. These included: in 1930, 20 inch instead of 21 inch wheels, in 1931 wider rear track, single point radiator mounting and thermostatically-controlled shutters, one-shot lubrication and improvements to brakes and front axle. In 1932 synchromesh was introduced on third and top gears and opening shutters to bonnet sides. In 1933 the characteristic Rolls-Royce throttle governor was unfortunately abandoned in favour of the more conventional hand-throttle. A new high-lift camshaft was introduced together with nitralloy crankshaft, new carburettor and air silencer; Luvax-Bijur fully-centralised chassis lubrication system; 28 gallon fuel tank; controllable shock absorbers ('ride control'); silent second gear; a new, more comfortable, thin-rimmed steering wheel and 19″ wheels. In 1934 a needle-bearing propeller shaft was introduced and in 1935 the low-lift camshaft was reintroduced and synchromesh was provided on second as well as third and top gears.

So it can be seen that by the UK series of 1935 the *Phantom II* had developed into a remarkably fine motor car, if a little old-fashioned. The short-chassis 'Continental' *Phantom II,* introduced to the public in 1933, was an even more desirable conveyance for the more sporting owner-driver. The prototype of this model was built especially for Sir Henry Royce in 1929, with a delightfully low-slung, close-coupled saloon body by Barker. The Rolls-Royce catalogue on these cars noted the following points about the chassis and coachwork:

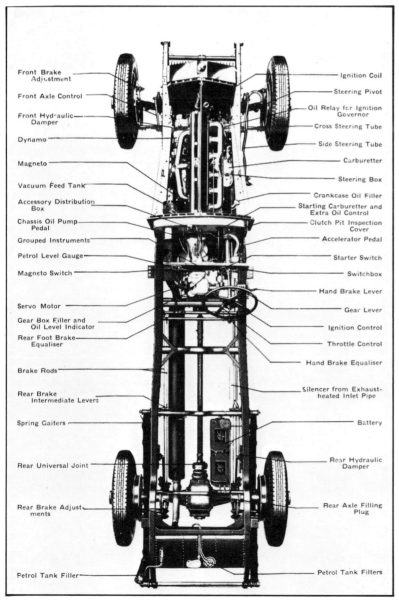

48. A plan view of the *Phantom II* chassis.

49. The Barker-bodied *Phantom II* made famous by M.G.M.'s film 'The Yellow Rolls-Royce'.

The chassis is a Phantom II short type with a specially low steering-column, specially selected springs of a type to permit of continuous high speeds over bad roads, supplemented with the standard Rolls-Royce patent hydraulic shock absorbers of the friction type.

Important modifications have recently been introduced to improve the speed, acceleration and performance generally. The compression ratio has been increased and the rear axle has a higher gear ratio.

The gearbox has a silent third speed and easy change mechanism as now standardised on all Rolls-Royce chassis.

The coachwork, a saloon of special design, having a sliding sun-shine roof, is a type which, as shown by experience, meets the requirements of the majority of those requiring a car for the purposes indicated.

THE PHANTOM II 'Continental'

The special features of the car are

LOW CENTRE OF GRAVITY

SUITABILITY FOR HIGH SPEED

LOW APPEARANCE

CLEAN EXTERNAL APPEARANCE

50. 1935 *Phantom II* Close-coupled Saloon with division by Thrupp & Maberly owned by Ian Bennett of Melbourne, Australia. Chassis No. 44UK.

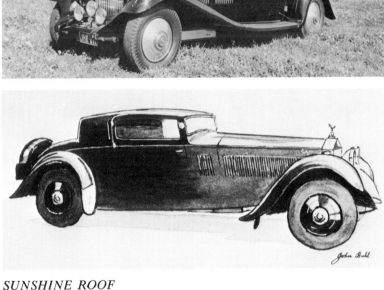

51. A delightful *Phantom II* Continental Sedanca-Coupé, by Gurney Nutting owned by Brian Healey of Melbourne, Australia. Chassis No. 60SK.

52. *Phantom II* Continental Razor-edged foursome Coupé by Freestone & Webb.

SUNSHINE ROOF
BUILT-IN LUGGAGE ACCOMMODATION

Ample head-room is maintained by the use of special cushions and by arranging the back seat in front of the upsweep of the chassis frame.

A luggage grid, invisible when not required, can also be provided at an extra charge. Thus the addition of this fitting does not adversely affect the external appearance of the car when the grid is not in use.

The complete car as described above was priced at £2,425. A *Phantom II* 7-passenger enclosed limousine was priced at £2,643 complete and an open tourer was £2,553. The chassis price was £1,850 for the short chassis and £1,900 for the long chassis. Complete cars were first offered by the Company on the *Phantom II* chassis in 1934.

53. A most attractive *Phantom II* Open Tourer, by Vanden Plas of Paris.
54. A magnificent *Phantom II* line-up in Jamestown, United States, 1963.

Phantom II Continental Performance Figures: *Autocar* August 1933.

Acceleration:

From rest to 50 m.p.h. through gears 14.6 secs

From rest to 60 m.p.h. through gears 19.6 secs

Best timed speed: 92.31 m.p.h.

Petrol consumption: 10-14 m.p.g.

Price in 1933: Park Ward Sports Saloon: £2,425

THE PHANTOM II
IN PRODUCTION 1929-1935

ENGINE

Six cylinders in two blocks of three, $4\frac{1}{4}$ inch bore by $5\frac{1}{2}$ inch stroke giving 7,668 c.c. and rated by the R.A.C. at 43.3 h.p. Overhead valves in aluminium head. Seven-bearing crankshaft with vibration damper. Twin-jet carburettor with starting carburettor, centrifugal governor. *1933* single-jet semi-expanding carburettor, no governor. *1935* large-choke carburettor.

CLUTCH

Single dry-plate type.

GEARBOX

Four speeds. *1932* synchromesh on third and fourth speeds. *1933* silent second gear. *1935* synchromesh second gear.

PROPELLER SHAFT

Open type with enclosed Universal joints. *1934* needle-bearing propeller shaft.

55. A *Phantom II* Continental Sports Saloon, by Hooper.

FINAL DRIVE

Fully-floating with hypoid bevel gears.

STEERING

Worm and nut.

SUSPENSION

Semi-elliptic front and rear.

1931 Split piston shock absorbers.

1933 'Ride control'. Continental chassis had Hartford shock absorbers with Andre telecontrol when specified.

BRAKES

Four-wheel system, servo-assisted.

PRINCIPAL DIMENSIONS

Overall length: 16' 8" short chassis; 17' 2" long chassis.

Wheelbase: 12' 0" short chassis; 12' 6" long chassis.

Track front: 4' 10½"; *1933*, 4' 10¾".

Track rear: 4' 10½"; *1931*, 5' 0"; *1933*, 5' 0¼".

NUMBER PRODUCED

1,767

CHASSIS SERIES

WJ, XJ, GN	1929-30	PY	1933-4
GY, GX	1930	RY, SK	1934
JS	1931-2	TA	1934-5
MS	1931-4	UK	1935
MY, MW	1933		

Certain chassis in the JS and MS series were left-hand drive chassis for the American market. These had an 'A' prefix ahead of the chassis letters e.g. 289 AJS.

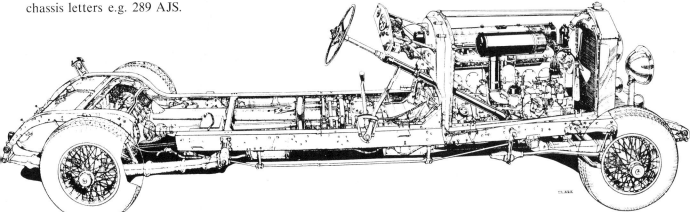

The Phantom III

The Rolls-Royce *Phantom III* introduced early in 1936 was, in the opinion of the author, the finest motor car of all time. This extravagant claim is fully justified by the refinement and sheer mechanical perfection of this magnificent car of cars. Unfortunately, the war curtailed its development and it was not reintroduced at the end of the hostilities.

It is not clear exactly when the decision to use a V-12 engine was taken, but the choice was a logical one in view of the Company's huge success with V-12 aero-engines. The practical advantage was that a higher-powered, smoother engine occupied a shorter space in the chassis. Twelve iron liners were inserted into an alloy cylinder block, cast as a sixty-degree vee formation, so that the outer surfaces of the liners were in contact with the coolant water. The two aluminium cylinder-heads carried overhead valves operated by push-rods from a camshaft mounted in the vee of the crankcase. At first the tappet settings were maintained hydraulically, but, as a result of blockage of the mechanism due mainly to negligence in cleaning the oil filters, many *Phantom III* engines suffered severe camshaft wear, so a change was made with the DL series of 1938 to a solid tappet design. Most of the earlier cars were recalled for conversion. This was unfortunate because given good, clean oil and regular routine maintenance the hydraulic-tappet engines give no trouble. The present day V-8, introduced in 1959 has a hydraulic-tappet arrangement of similar design to that of the *Phantom III*.

Another admirable feature of the *Phantom III*, also removed with the DL series, was the heat-exchanger unit, consisting of a matrix on the side of the sump which used coolant water to maintain the oil temperature at a constant level and to warm it quickly following a cold start. This feature also fell victim to poor maintenance and its abolition corresponded with the introduction of Hall's metal big-ends.

The earliest prototype engines were equipped with four carburettors mounted above the vee of the engine but production versions had a single duplex down-draught type.

As with previous *Phantoms*, a dual ignition system was provided, comprising two coils, two distributors and no fewer than twenty-four sparking plugs! One distributor supplied the twelve plugs on the inlet side of the heads while the other distributor supplied those on the exhaust side. One side of the system was timed to fire slightly ahead of the other for more efficient combustion.

As on previous models a set of relief valves fed oil to the crankshaft at 25-35 p.s.i., the valve rocker shafts at 10 p.s.i. and the timing gears at $1\frac{3}{4}$ p.s.i.

The *Phantom III* was the first Rolls-Royce to have independent front suspension. This system, based on the General Motors principle,

56. A *Phantom III* Sports Saloon by Park Ward.

57. A 1937 *Phantom III* Sports Saloon with division by H.J. Mulliner. Owned by Jim Matches of Melbourne, Australia. Chassis No. 3CP82.

58. *Phantom III* Sedanca-de-Ville by Hooper.

59. *Phantom III* Limousine-de-Ville by Hooper.

60. *Phantom III* Sedanca-de-Ville by Gurney Nutting.

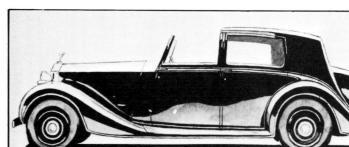

61. 1938. *Phantom III* Sedanca-de-Ville by H. J. Mulliner.

62. 1939 *Phantom III* Sedanca-de-Ville by H. J. Mulliner.

consisted of a 'wishbone' lever system controlled by coil springs and hydraulic dampers enclosed in oil-filled housings. The absence of heavy dumb-irons and leaf-springs at the front end of the chassis enabled the radiator and engine to be moved forward, enabling exceedingly spacious coachwork to be mounted on a shortened chassis. Each leaf of the semi-elliptic rear springs was ground to size and fitted together on its end surfaces. In addition, by means of a series of oil holes and grooves the three longest leaves were lubricated by oil from the one-shot system. The springs were, of course, enclosed in the usual leather gaiters.

With all the new features the *Phantom III* was a very advanced motor car, and as such was the first really radical departure from the *Silver Ghost*. Today a good *Phantom III* is a highly desirable car although many enthusiasts are shy of them because of their mechanical complexity and the resultant expense of repair work. A complete *Phantom III* engine overhaul carried out by Rolls-Royce Ltd, or by one of their special retailers leaves its owner with little change out of £2,000.

Phantom III Performance Figures:

'Autocar' October 1936.

Acceleration:

From rest to 30 m.p.h. through gears 5.5 secs.
  ,,   ,,   ,, 50 m.p.h.   ,,   ,,   12.6 ,,
  ,,   ,,   ,, 60 m.p.h.   ,,   ,,   16.8 ,,
  ,,   ,,   ,, 70 m.p.h.   ,,   ,,   24.4 ,,

Best timed speed: 91.84 m.p.h.

Maximum speeds in gears:

2nd: 44 m.p.h.

3rd: 73 m.p.h.

Petrol consumption: 10 m.p.g.

Price in 1936:

Barker Touring Limousine: £2,615

Park Ward Pullman Limousine: £2,600

Chassis: £1,800

63. Owen Bailey's 1938 *Phantom III* Sedanca Drophead Coupé by Gurney Nutting. Chassis No. 3AZ158.

THE PHANTOM III
IN PRODUCTION 1936-1939

ENGINE

Twelve cylinders arranged in 60° vee, $3\frac{1}{4}$ inch bore by $4\frac{1}{2}$ inch stroke giving 7,340 c.c. and rated by the R.A.C. at 50.7 h.p. Overhead valves in aluminium head, operated from single camshaft mounted in the vee of the crankcase. *1936*, hydraulic tappets. *1938*, solid tappets. Duplex down-draught carburettor.

CLUTCH

Single dry-plate type.

GEARBOX

1936 Four-speeds. Synchromesh on 2nd, 3rd, and 4th.
1938 Overdrive fourth speed.

PROPELLER SHAFT

Open type with enclosed needle-bearing universal joints.

FINAL DRIVE

Fully-floating with hypoid spiral bevel gears.

STEERING

Worm and sector.

SUSPENSION

Independent front with enclosed coil-springs, semi-elliptic rear. Hydraulic shock dampers with 'ride control'.

BRAKES

Four-wheel system servo-assisted.

PRINCIPAL DIMENSIONS

Overall length: 17' 7"
Wheelbase: 11' 10"
Track front: 5' 0.6"
Track rear: 5' 2.6"

PRICE

Chassis £1,900. Complete cars from £2,587 for a *Sports Tourer* to £2,870 for a *Sedanca de Ville*.

CHASSIS NUMBERS

3AZ20-238, 3AX1-201	1936	3CP2-200, 3CM1-203	1937-8
3BU2-200, 3BT1-203	1937	3DL2-200, 3DH1-9	1938-9
		Total 710	

At least four *Phantom III's* with 'experimental department' chassis numbers are known to exist e.g. 3DEX202, owned by Mr John Griffiths of Melbourne, Australia. The number 13 was not used in any series.

64. *Phantom III* with Park Ward coachwork and altered wingline by Jack Barclay Ltd. This car is now in Australia and owned by Mr Bill Fagan. Chassis No. 3DL108.

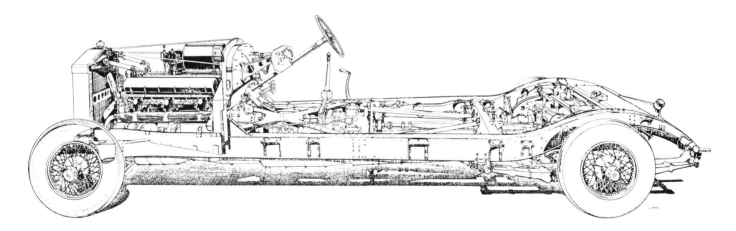

The Small Rolls-Royce

In 1922 the Company announced that a new, smaller model was to be produced alongside the *Ghost*. This confirmed the 'Baby Rolls-Royce' rumours that had cropped up from time to time.

The small model, known as the *Twenty Horsepower,* differed from the *Silver Ghost* in many respects other than size. The *Twenty* engine was a six-cylinder unit of 3,127 c.c. capacity, with pushrod operated overhead valves. The gearbox had only three forward speeds and the change-lever was centrally mounted, together with the hand-brake lever. Suspension was by semi-elliptic springs all round. In this form the *Twenty* was a very pleasant and charming car indeed but although the legendary Rolls-Royce top-gear flexibility was apparent the three-speed box did not meet with acceptance. The central ball-type change was not in the Rolls-Royce tradition; in fact it was at that time un-English and more commonly to be seen in cars of Trans-Atlantic origin. In 1925 a change was made to a four-speed gearbox with a delightful right-hand gate-type change.

At first two-wheel brakes were fitted to the *Twenty* but by 1925 four-wheel brakes with gearbox-driven servo were offered.

Unlike that of the *Silver Ghost,* the radiator of the *Twenty* had shutters controlled from the instrument panel. At first these were horizontal and enamelled but later versions had nickel-silver shutters and by 1928 vertical shutters were fitted to conform with the *Phantom I.* The mascot used was a smaller (5 inches) version of the *Silver Ghost* mascot.

The *Twenty* is not by any means a high-performance car, but, having a certain charm that makes it quite unlike other Rolls-Royce models, it has a faithful following of enthusiasts who clearly prefer it to the *Silver Ghost* and *Phantom I.* Certainly the small model is more easily maintained in good order and, of course, it consumes far less fuel.

Over the years the *Twenty* developed into the 20/25 h.p., introduced in 1929. The early 20/25's were almost identical to the late *Twenties* except that the cylinder bore was increased by $\frac{1}{4}$ inch to $3\frac{1}{4}$ inch giving a capacity of 3,699 c.c. This was the first of a series of bore increases of the small six-cylinder engine culminating in the *Silver Cloud* of 1955 with a bore of no less than $3\frac{3}{4}$ inches, which still retained the same centre-to-centre dimension of 4.15 inches.

From a performance aspect the larger engine capacity of the 20/25 makes it immediately more desirable than the *Twenty,* with absolutely no sacrifice of the typical Rolls-Royce silence, docility and ease of control. As with its larger contemporary, the *Phantom II,* many improvements were made to the 20/25 over the seven years it was in production.

These improvements are outlined as follows:

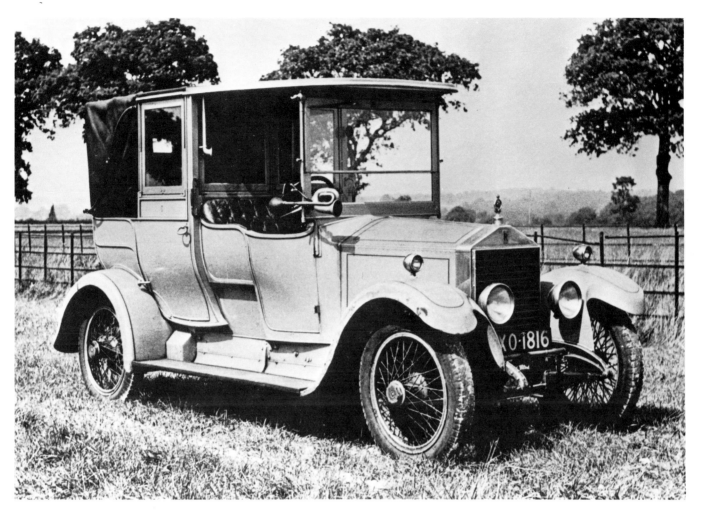

1930 Flexible engine suspension
      5.25: 1 compression ratio
      Longer wheelbase (11′ 0″)
1931 Reserve petrol supply
1932 Completely centralised chassis lubrication system
      Diamond engine mounting
      New thin-rimmed steering wheel
      Improved engine performance, 5.75: 1 compression ratio
      High-lift camshaft
      Double-acting hydraulic shock dampers
      Larger radiator
      'Staybrite' radiator shell
      Thermostatically-controlled shutters
      Low-inertia spring-drive crankshaft vibration damper
      Two-rate charging system
      Electric fuel gauge
      Synchromesh on third and top gears
1933 Nitralloy crankshaft
      Three-rate charging system
      Silent second gear
1934 Single-jet expanding carburettor
      Air silencer

65. 1923 20 h.p. with earlier coachwork (1910 ex-Daimler). Originally owned by the Earl of Lonsdale and appropriately finished in the famous Lonsdale Yellow! Now part of the Sears Collection.

41

66. Rolls-Royce 20/25 h.p. early series.
67. A line-up of 25/30 h.p. Rolls-Royce cars at the second Western Meet, June 1964.

Needle-bearing propeller shaft
Ride control
D.W.S. permanent screw jacks
1935 Flexible engine mounting
Voltage-controlled generator
1936 Borg & Beck clutch
Hypoid rear axle
Marles cam & roller steering

68. Rolls-Royce 20 h.p. Open Tourer.

20/25 h.p. Performance Figures: *Autocar* June 1935.
Acceleration:
From rest to 50 m.p.h. through gears 21.0 secs.
  ,,   ,,   ,, 60 m.p.h.   ,,   ,,   31.4 ,,
Best timed speed: 76.27 m.p.h.
Maximum speeds in gears:
1st: 18 m.p.h.
2nd: 32 m.p.h.
3rd: 53 m.p.h.
Petrol consumption: Driven hard — 14 m.p.g.
Price in 1935:
Hooper close-coupled Sports Saloon: £1,658

In 1936, the bore of the engine was increased to 3½ inches giving a capacity of 4,257 c.c. The resultant more powerful car was called the 25/30 h.p. and for a short time after its introduction the 20/25 was still available as an alternative. Apart from being larger the engine of the 25/30 differed from that of the 20/25 by its Stromberg carburettor fed by twin S.U. electric fuel pumps mounted on the bulkhead. The 25/30 may be instantly distinguished from a late 20/25 by its three-spoked steering wheel, later examples having the flat Phantom III-type boss and horn button.

Although the increased power from the larger engine enabled the car to reach 80 m.p.h., top gear flexibility was unimpaired.

69. *Above* Rolls-Royce 20/25 h.p. four-seater Coupé with coachwork by Park Ward.

70. 1926 20 h.p. Park Ward Saloon with owner Terry Bruce at the wheel. Chassis No. GYK 47.

71. Sports Saloon built by Hooper on the 20/25 h.p. chassis.

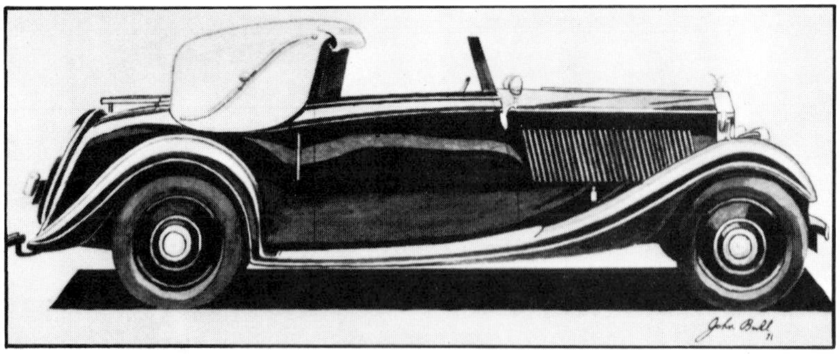

72. Gurney Nutting's Sedanca Coupé. The example shown here is on the 20/25 h.p. chassis.

THE TWENTY HORSEPOWER IN PRODUCTION 1922–1929

ENGINE

Six cylinders in one block, 3 inch bore by 4½ inch stroke giving

3,127 c.c. and rated by the R.A.C. at 21.6 h.p. Overhead valves in cast iron head, operated from camshaft by pushrods. Seven bearing crankshaft with 'Slipper flywheel' vibration damper. Twin-jet carburettor and starting carburettor. Hand throttle on steering column quadrant. Coil ignition with stand-by magneto. Electric starter.

CLUTCH

Single dry-plate.

GEARBOX

Unit construction with engine.

1922 three speeds with centre change lever.

1925 four speeds with right-hand lever.

PROPELLER SHAFT

Open shaft.

FINAL DRIVE

Fully floating rear axle with spiral bevel final drive.

STEERING

Worm and nut.

SUSPENSION

1922 Semi-elliptic front and rear with friction shock absorbers.

1926 Hydraulic front shock absorbers.

1928 Hydraulic all round.

BRAKES

1922 Rear drums. *1925* Four wheel servo assisted system available.

PRINCIPAL DIMENSIONS

Overall length: 14′ 10″

Wheelbase: 10′ 9″

Track: 4′ 6″

CHASSIS SERIES

20 h.p.		GEX, GWX, GDX,	
G, S, H, A, K, GA, GF,		GSY, GLZ, GTZ,	
GH, GAK, GMK, GRK,		GYZ, GBA, GGA,	
GDK, GLK, GNK	1922-5	GHA.	1933
GPK, GSK	1925-6	GXB, GUB, GLB,	
GCK, GOK, GZK,		GNC, GRC, GKC,	
GUK, GYK	1926	GED, GMD, GYD,	
GMJ, GHJ, GAJ	1926-7	GAE, GWE, GFE,	1934
GRJ, GUJ	1927	GAF, GSF, GRF	1934–5
GXL, GYL, GWL,		GLG, GPG, GHG,	
GBM, GKM, GTM	1928	GYH, GOH, GEH,	
GFN, GLN	1928–9	GBJ, GLJ, GCJ	1935
GEN, GVO, GXO	1929	GXK, GBK, GTK	1936
Total 2,940		Total 3,827	
20/25 h.p.		25/30 h.p.	
GXO	1929–30	GUL, GTL, GHL,	
GGP, GDP, GWP,		GRM, GXM, GGM,	
GLR, GSR, GTR	1930	GAN, GWN, GUN	1936–7
GNS, GOS, GPS	1930–1	GRO, GHO, GMO,	
GFT, GBT, GKT	1931–2	GRP, GMP, GLP	1937
GAU, GMU, GZU	1932	GAR, GGR, GZR	1937–8
GHW, GRW, GAW	1932–3	Total 1,201	

The Silent Sports Car

Under Rolls-Royce Ltd the Bentley company became 'Bentley Motors (1931) Ltd' and production of Bentley cars was recommenced in 1933 at the Derby works. The first model produced by the new company was the '3½-litre', developed by matching a twin S.U. carburettor version of the 20/25 h.p. engine to the 10 foot 6 inch wheelbase chassis of the experimental 18 h.p. model, known at the works as the 'Peregrine'. A handful of the famous 3-litre model was turned out from spares acquired from the old company.

The new model, first introduced to the public in August 1933, was an instant success and quickly became known as the 'Silent Sports Car', a title which speaks worlds of the inimitably silent high performance so characteristic of the Bentley car as produced by Rolls-Royce Ltd.

A great many widely-varying styles of coachwork executed by a number of British and Continental coachbuilders were offered on the 3½-litre chassis, ranging from the sportiest of two-seaters to rather too-heavy saloons, a few of which were oddly equipped with divisions between front and rear compartments. When unencumbered by heavy coachwork the performance of the 3½-litre left nothing to be desired, the top speed being in excess of 90 m.p.h. However, performance naturally suffered a little when the chassis was forced to carry incongruous, bulky coachwork. This unfortunate situation was largely overcome in 1936 when a twin carburettor version of the 4,257 c.c. 25/30 h.p. engine became available in the Bentley chassis. This model was known as the 4¼-litre, the 3½-litre remaining in production for a year or so. With the MR series of 1939 an overdrive fourth gearbox was introduced for the 4¼-litre, enabling even more effortless high-speed cruising to be indulged in without fear of overworking the engine.

1939 saw the introduction of independent front suspension in the Bentley chassis with the *Mk V* model, which never went into series production because of the war. The exact number of *Mk V's* built is not known but the figure is believed to have been fewer than twenty. Only seven examples are known to have survived.

A special modified version of the *Mk V* was sent to the coachbuilder Van Vooren of Paris to be fitted with a streamlined sports saloon body which departed from tradition in that the Bentley radiator shell was replaced by a streamlined, though rather ugly, cowling. This car, in which no ingredient for effortless high-speed travel was lacking and for which series production was envisaged, was called the *Corniche.* Unfortunately, only her ignition keys survived a German bomb attack on the docks of Dieppe.

Another *Mk V* was fitted with a post-war *Phantom IV*-type straight-eight engine and called the *Scalded Cat.* One wonders what

wonderful machinery may have been introduced to the public had the war not intervened.

73. 1938 *Bentley* 4¼-litre Saloon. Coach builder not known but probably Park Ward.
74. 1934 *Bentley* 3½-litre Drophead Coupé.

PRE-WAR BENTLEYS
IN PRODUCTION 1933–1941

ENGINE

Six cylinders in one block, 3¼ inch bore by 4½ inch stroke giving 3,669 c.c. and rated by the R.A.C. at 25.3 h.p. *1936* 3½ inch bore by 4½ inch stroke giving 4,257 c.c. and rated by the R.A.C. at 29.4 h.p. Pushrod operated overhead valves. Seven bearing crankshaft with vibration damper. Twin S.U. carburettors with mixture and hand-throttle controls on steering column. Battery ignition with automatic timing with overriding control on steering column.

75. *Bentley* 4¼-litre Sedanca Coupé by James Young.

76. *Bentley* 4¼-litre Sports Saloon by H.J. Mulliner.

77. *Bentley* 3½-litre Drophead Coupé. Coachwork by Martin & King of Melbourne, Australia. Owned by Dennis Manley of the United Kingdom. Chassis No. B83BN.

78. *Top Bentley* 4¼-litre Vanden Plas 'Weather' (B104JD). Owned by Ted Reich, U.S.A.

79. *Above* 1938 4¼-litre *Bentley* Tourer, coachwork by Park Ward.

80. *Left Bentley* 4¼-litre Drophead Coupé by Thrupp & Maberly.

81. Dennis Manley's 3½-litre *Bentley* Drophead Coupé with coachwork by Martin & King of Melbourne, Australia.

82. 1935 *Bentley* 3½-litre 'Airflow Saloon' by Thrupp & Maberly.

83. *Bentley* 4¼-litre Sedanca Coupé by J. Gurney Nutting.

84. An attractive two door Saloon by H.J. Mulliner on the 4¼-litre *Bentley* chassis.

CLUTCH
Single dry-plate.

GEARBOX
1933 Four forward speeds with direct drive on top.
1939 Overdrive on fourth.

PROPELLER SHAFT
Open shaft with universal joints.
1936 Needle-bearing universal joints.

FINAL DRIVE
1933 Fully-floating rear axle with hypoid gears.
Corniche model: semi-floating axle.

STEERING
1933 Worm and nut.
1936 Marles cam and roller.

SUSPENSION
1933 Semi-elliptics all round.
1934 Hydraulic shock dampers with 'ride control'.
1939 Independent front suspension by coil springs.

BRAKES
Four-wheel system, servo-assisted.

PRINCIPAL DIMENSIONS
Overall length:	*1933*	14' 6"
	1939	15' 11"
Wheelbase:	*1933*	10' 6"
	1939	10' 4"
Track:	*1933*	4' 8"
	1939	Front: 4' 8½"
		Rear: 4' 10"

NUMBERS PRODUCED
3½-litre	1,191. Chassis series AE, AH, BL, BN, CR, CW, DG, DK, EF, EJ, FB, FC
4½-litre	1,241. Chassis series GA, GP, HK, HM, JD, JY, KT, KU, LS, LE, MR, MX
Mk. V	Believed 17. Chassis series AW
Corniche	Only one or possibly two. Only known chassis number 14BV

The 25/30h.p. 'Wraith'

The 25/30 h.p. *Wraith* model, with independent front suspension, was announced in October 1938. Although it may, at first sight, appear to be merely a modified 25/30 the *Wraith* was in fact an entirely new model which brought the design of the 'small' Rolls-Royce into line with that of its larger counterpart, the mighty *Phantom III*.

Apart from the obvious improvement incorporated in the *Wraith* (including the *Phantom III*-style independent front suspension with fully enclosed coil springs and shock dampers), numerous other changes distinguished it from its predecessor, the 25/30 h.p. Most important of these improvements is the redesigned 4,257 c.c. engine which differed from that of the 25/30 by having the inlet and exhaust manifolds mounted on opposite sides of the head, a water jacket being provided to heat the inlet manifold. The valves were much larger and were operated, through pushrods and rockers, by barrel-type tappets which were designed to rotate to ensure sufficient lubrication and even wear. The redesigned ignition system incorporated a spare coil, and a better timing governor enabling the elimination of the traditional 'Early and Late' hand control on the steering wheel.

The actual chassis frame was completely redesigned, being welded instead of riveted. The deep box-section side members were pierced to reduce the weight and braced by a very substantial cruciform member in the centre and by transverse members at the front and rear ends.

Alterations to the steering mechanism made the car considerably lighter to control while the right-hand mounted gear lever and brake lever were moved further back in the chassis so that they offered no obstruction to entry and exit through the driver's door.

To expedite wheel-changing, the *Wraith* was equipped with a D.W.S. permanent hydraulic jacking system controlled by valves under the floor of the front compartment.

The lengthened (11' 4") wheelbase enabled the *Wraith* chassis to carry larger, more commodious coachwork than hitherto.

The chassis price was unchanged at £1,100 while complete cars were available at prices ranging from £1,610 for a saloon with sunshine roof to £1,660 for a touring limousine with division and heater and £1,885 for a special saloon with division and heater. It is a great pity that only 491 chassis were produced before the war put a stop to production.

THE 25/30 h.p. 'WRAITH'
IN PRODUCTION 1938–1939

ENGINE

Six cylinders in one block, 3½ inch bore by 4½ inch stroke giving

85. 1939 *Wraith* Sports Saloon with coachwork by Freestone & Webb.
86. 1939 25/30 h.p. Rolls-Royce *Wraith* Pullman Limousine.

87. The *Wraith* gearbox.

88. The *Wraith* engine with head removed.

4,257 c.c. and rated by the R.A.C. at 29.4 h.p. Overhead valves operated by pushrods. Seven-bearing crankshaft with vibration damper. Fixed jet downdraught carburettor. Hand-throttle on steering column quadrant. Battery ignition, fully automatic timing.

CLUTCH
   Single dry-plate.

GEARBOX
   Four speeds with right-hand change.

PROPELLER SHAFT
   Totally enclosed needle roller bearing universal joints.

FINAL DRIVE
   Fully floating rear axle with hypoid gears.

STEERING
   Marles cam and roller.

SUSPENSION
   Independent front suspension by coil springs and hydraulic dampers totally enclosed in oil-filled housings. Rear suspension by semi-elliptics and hydraulic shock dampers. 'Ride control.'

BRAKES
   Four-wheel servo-assisted system.

89. 1939 *Wraith* two door Saloon by James Young. Owned by Russell Rolls, Victoria, Australia. Chassis No. WMB38.

90. 1939 *Wraith* Razor-edge Saloon by H.J. Mulliner.

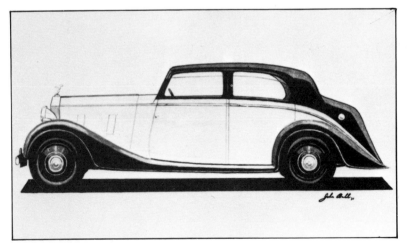

91. The Sports Saloon on a *Wraith* chassis by Greenstone & Webb.

92. 1939 Rolls-Royce *Wraith* Saloon with division by H.J. Mulliner.

PRINCIPAL DIMENSIONS
  Overall length: 16′ 11″
  Wheelbase: 11′ 4″
  Track, front: 4′ 10½″
  Track, rear: 4′ 11½″

CHASSIS NUMBERS

WXA1–109	1938	WHC1–81, WEC1–81,	
WRB1–81, WMB1–81,		WKC1–24	1939
WLB1–41	1938–9	Total 491	

World War II

Adolf Hitler's fanatical greed for power was responsible for halting the development of three very promising cars, the *Phantom III*, the *Wraith* and the *Mk. V* Bentley (which was never actually released to the public). All Rolls-Royce manufacturing plants were engaged in the manufacture of the famous aero-engines, and various other engines for military purposes. The list of aeroplanes and military vehicles powered by Rolls-Royce would be too long to include here, but the Avro Lancaster Bomber and the Spitfire and Hurricane Fighters were the most notable World War II aircraft powered by Rolls-Royce. Development of motor car engines continued through the war and Rolls-Royce were able to recover in time to introduce a new car by 1946 with a revised version of the pre-war $4\frac{1}{4}$-litre, six cylinder engine.

93. *Wraith* Seven-passenger Limousine by Park Ward 1938-1939.

Post-War Engines

The *'B'* series engines, developed during the war from the pre-war *Wraith* and Bentley engines, were used from 1946 in three forms: the *B40* (four cylinder, used for the Austin *Champ*); the *B60* (six cylinder, introduced in refined form in 1946 for the *Mk. VI* Bentley, and for the *Silver Wraith* in 1947) and the *B80* (employed in heavy vehicles, but not in a motor car until 1950 when the straight-eight *Phantom IV* was introduced).

We need only deal here with the six, but it will be noted that the straight-eight was basically similar. Only eighteen straight-eight *Phantoms* were built.

When comparing a post-war 4¼-litre engine to its pre-war equivalent the most notable difference lies in the valve layout. When the 4¼-litre engine appeared in 1936 the valve openings were comparatively small, and the demand for larger valves out-grew the space available for overhead valves. The answer lay in a reversion to Royce's arrangement, 'F'-head, or overhead inlet, side exhaust valve layout. The passing of gear-trains in favour of vee-belts for the generator and water pump drive was harshly criticised. However, the use of belts meant that the engineers were faced with fewer problems concerning noise and proved quite acceptable thanks to vast improvements in modern belt materials.

The 'F'-head 4¼-litre engine lasted five years before an increase in capacity to 4,566 c.c. took place. This modification was made possible only after the engineers at Crewe were able to develop pistons which would safely run in cylinders without water-spaces. The increased acceleration of cars fitted with the 'big-bore' engine was very noticeable.

94. Section through a post-war inlet-over-exhaust ('F-head') engine clearly showing the valve layout and oil circulation.

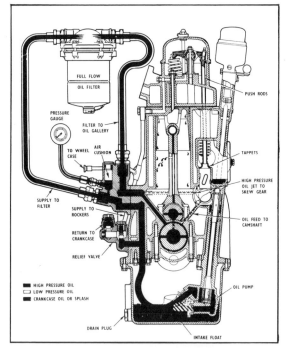

A New Bentley with Standardised Coachwork

The Company resumed motor car production at Crewe in 1946, with, at first, only one model known as the *Mk. VI* Bentley. Much to the delight of the untiring band of critics, the new model was produced with all-steel bodywork assembled and finished in specially-built workshops adjoining the factory. The steel panels were supplied in a raw state by the Pressed Steel Company of Birmingham, a firm well-known as the producer of the body panels of practically every British car made with steel coachwork. This highly practical new policy led to complaints to the effect that a Rolls-Royce (whether masquerading as a Bentley or not) with pressed-steel standardised body was not what the customers wanted, or expected from such a prestige company as Rolls-Royce. However, despite heavy taxation of the wealthy, due mainly to political upheaval following the costly business of winning the war, the new cars sold reasonably well at first and, even before the *Silver Cloud* was announced, more standard saloons had been sold than *Silver Ghosts*.

However, for those who preferred special coachwork, and to ride a little more sedately behind Charles Sykes' 'Spirit of Ecstasy', the *Silver Wraith* was available with a choice of Saloon, Limousine, Sedanca-de-Ville or Drophead Coupé coachwork by any one of five different British coachbuilders. When the success of the Standard Steel Saloon was established, the doom of the coachbuilders was predicted. It was thought that with their traditional materials and craftsmen's methods, they could not possibly survive in a modern world. The passage of time proved these prophets to be, to a certain extent, quite accurate in their predictions, and both Hooper (Coachbuilders) Ltd, and Freestone & Webb had ceased to exist by 1959. It was a great pity that Hooper's never survived to build coachwork for the *Phantom V* in greater numbers. H. J. Mulliner-Park Ward Ltd, owned and controlled today by Rolls-Royce, and James Young Ltd, were together producing fewer than 350 bodies per year by 1964. Previously H. J. Mulliner and Park Ward were independent both of each other and of Rolls-Royce Ltd, but nowadays they share the same premises in Willesden. James Young Ltd, as a subsidiary of the Jack Barclay organisation, closed down as the last surviving privately-owned coachbuilder for Rolls-Royce and Bentley cars.

Unlike the coachbuilt cars, and despite elaborate rustproofing techniques, the standard bodies are not immune from rust, and it is not at all unusual to find a fifteen year old Rolls-Royce or Bentley rusting quite badly, usually through neglect. The obvious advantage of standardised steel coachwork is the cost at which it can be produced in comparatively large numbers; a Rolls-Royce or Bentley with specialised coachwork currently costs about 30 per cent more than a standard saloon. Nowadays the coachbuilder's clients are restricted to those individualists 'who require a car of particular distinction', usually a limousine, sports saloon or drophead coupé.

95. *Bentley MK. VI* Four door Sports Saloon. Coachwork by Bentley Motors (1931) Ltd.
96. 1951 *Bentley MK. VI.*

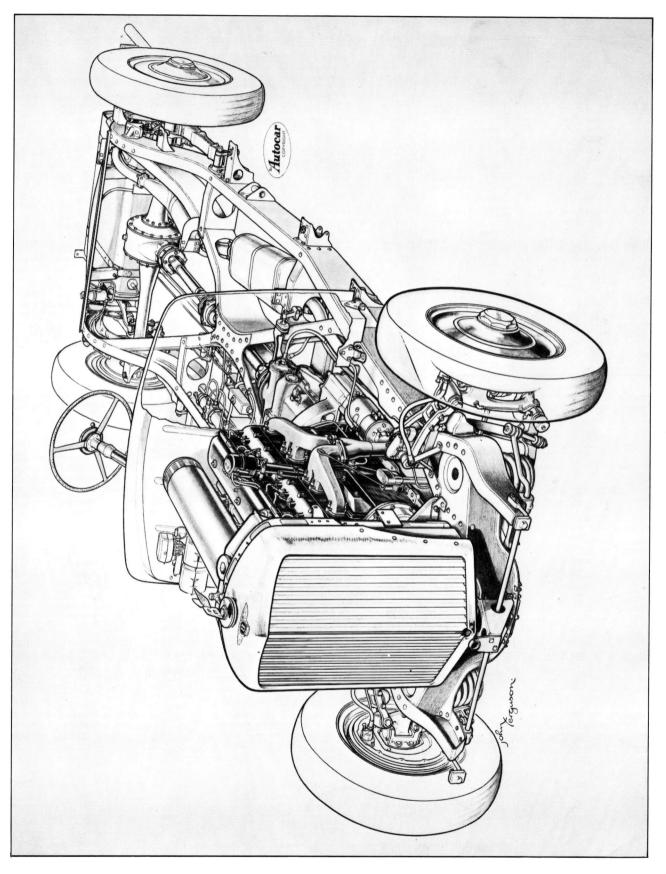

97. The *Bentley MK. VI* chassis.

98. 1948 *Bentley MK. VI* Sports Saloon by James Young. This is one of James Young's first post-war designs and closely resembles some of their late pre-war Rolls-Royce designs.

99. An unusual design by Gurney Nutting known as the 'Teardrop' Coupé, 1950

100. 1950 *Bentley MK. VI* James Young two door Saloon.
101. 1950 *Bentley MK. VI* Coupé-de-Ville by James Young.

102. 1952 *Bentley MK. VI.* Saloon by James Young. This beautiful coachwork was also available in two door form.
103. 1952 *Bentley MK. VI.* two door Saloon by James Young.

104. *Bentley MK. VI.* with Freestone & Webb coachwork.

105. *Bentley MK. VI.* Sports Saloon by H.J. Mulliner.

106. Hooper four door Sports Saloon (Design No. 8294) on *Bentley MK. VI* and 'R'-type chassis. Introduced in 1952.

107. *Bentley MK. VI* Coupé by H.J. Mulliner.

108. *Bentley MK. VI.* Coupé by Franay of Paris.

The Rolls-Royce Automatic Gearbox

As from 1952 all Rolls-Royce and Bentley cars were available with the new automatic transmission. Previously the Rolls-Royce gearbox was of the four-speed synchromesh pattern and had the distinction of being controlled by a lever mounted on the floor on the right hand side of the driver (excepting, of course, left-hand drive models which were equipped with a column mounted lever).

The design of the Rolls-Royce automatic transmission was borrowed (like that of independent front suspension) from the General Motors Corporation, whose 'Hydramatic' was found by Rolls-Royce engineers to be the best available at the time. A great many refinements were made to the original design and at one stage a rough spot was machined to Rolls-Royce tolerances resulting in the unit completely ceasing to function! It is of the hydraulic coupling and epicyclic gear type, and changes in ratio are brought about by means of hydraulic servo mechanisms. As fitted to all models up to the latest *Silver Shadow* and its equivalent Bentley the column-mounted selector was an admirably simple mechanism enabling the driver to select the required gear range. When left in position 4 all changes of ratio are left to the 'brain' third or second being available for quick bursts of acceleration or for engine braking on steep hills. A safety device protecting the engine from over-revving automatically effects a change from third to top at peak revs, and thus no damage is caused by making the easy mistake of not changing back to fourth after employing the 'hold third' position. Reverse gear and neutral cannot be selected until a small button in the end of the lever is depressed. No 'Park' position as such is provided but by selecting reverse and turning off the engine two gears are engaged together— a highly effective parking lock.

Since its introduction in 1952, the automatic transmission has undergone constant improvement. The editor of the monthly magazine *Motor Sport* was of the opinion that, *I have experienced smoother automatic gearboxes, although the Chief Engineer of Rolls-Royce explains the quite vicious kick you experience if open throttles catch the gearbox out before it is in low gear by saying that it is the biggest unsolved problem confronting users of this particular form of automatic transmission.* In its latest form the range selection is electrically effected from a redesigned lever and quadrant, an innovation which is dealt with in a subsequent section on the *Silver Shadow*.

109. Rolls-Royce automatic gearbox.

The 'R'-Type Bentley

In 1952, by lengthening the chassis, the *Mk. VI* Bentley evolved into the *'R'* series. The extra length enabled the Bentley (and Rolls-Royce *Silver Dawn*) to assume a more handsome, balanced appearance, together with the advantage of extra luggage space. The Rolls-Royce automatic gearbox was available (for export only at first) on the 'R' type as an option, and by 1954 was a standard fitting.

THE BENTLEY CONTINENTAL

The distinguished title *Continental* was first bestowed upon the special short-chassis *Phantom II* of 1931, (the prototype of which Royce used as his personal transport) and was revived in 1951 for a new streamlined Bentley speedster. The 'R' type Bentley *Continental* was designed by John Bletchley and H. I. F. Evernden, the latter being the original designer of the *Phantom II Continental*. Every care was taken in the car's design to maintain weight at a minimum; a tuned engine and higher gearing enabled the car to attain a maximum speed in the region of 120 m.p.h. when carrying the aerodynamic coachwork by H. J. Mulliner which was fitted to all but sixteen examples.

Co-operation between Rolls-Royce Ltd and H. J. Mulliner resulted in a sleek, beautiful two-door sports saloon, a genuine Gran Turismo, with a lower radiator shell designed by Mulliners to blend with their coachwork. The curved, sharply-raked windscreen and gently sloping 'fast-back' roofline provided the essential impression of speed. *Continental* customers had the choice of Rolls-Royce four-speed automatic transmission (from 1954), or synchromesh gearbox with the traditional right-hand lever. The prototype *Continental* was at first fitted with an overdrive gearbox.

The *'D'* series *Continental* appeared in 1954 with a 4,887 c.c. engine evolved by boring out yet again to $3\frac{3}{4}$ inches.

BENTLEY MK. VI and 'R'-TYPE
IN PRODUCTION 1946-1955

ENGINE

Six cylinders in line. *1946* Bore $3\frac{1}{2}$ inches, stroke $4\frac{1}{2}$ inches, 4,257 c.c. 29.4 h.p. (R.A.C. rating). *1951* Bore $3\frac{5}{8}$ inches, stroke $4\frac{1}{2}$ inches; 4,566 c.c. 31.5 h.p. (R.A.C. rating). *1954 Continental* Bore $3\frac{3}{4}$ inches, stroke $4\frac{1}{2}$ inches; 4,887 c.c. 33.7 h.p. (R.A.C. rating). Overhead inlet, side exhaust valves, aluminium cylinder head, twin S.U. carburettors (L.H. drive *Mk. VI's* had single Stromberg), twin S.U. fuel pumps.

GEARBOX

Four speed and reverse, synchromesh on second, third and top gears, side control (column control on L.H. drive cars).

110. 1952 'R'-type *Bentley* Saloon, as it appears in the catalogue.
111. 'R'-type *Bentley* standard steel Saloon. This design, with longer tail, was introduced in 1952 and was available with automatic transmission.

BENTLEY

SPORTS SALOON

The Sports Saloon coachwork by Bentley Motors (1931) Ltd. is in keeping with the quality of the chassis and retains the air of a thoroughbred in the true Bentley tradition. In addition to its beauty of line, the design of the body is essentially practical. The car will seat four or five passengers in great comfort whilst the luggage accommodation provided in the boot is very considerable.

The interior finish creates an air of unostentatious luxury. All the fittings illustrated are supplied at no extra charge and include a radio, hot and cold air ventilation and de-misting, electrically operated de-misting for the rear window and companion sets in the rear compartment. The interior and exterior of these cars may be finished in a variety of colour schemes.

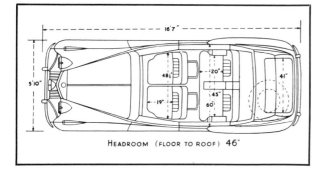

112. Advertising for the *Bentley* Sports Saloon from the 1953 Bentley catalogue.
113. 'Olga'—Stanley Sedgwick's prototype 'R' Continental, originally known as *Corniche II*. Chassis No. BC26A.

114. 'R'-type *Bentley* two door Sports Saloon by James Young.
115. 'R'-type *Bentley* four door Saloon by James Young.

Ratios: *Mk. VI 1st,* 2.99: 1, *2nd,* 2.05: 1, *3rd,* 1.33: 1, *Top,* 1: 1
'R' Type 1st, 3.8: 1, *2nd,* 2.34: 1, *3rd,* 1.28: 1, *Top,* 1: 1
Continental 1st, 2.64: 1, *2nd,* 1.55: 1, *3rd,* 1.22: 1, *Top,* 1: 1

Rolls-Royce automatic gearbox available on 'R' Type.

TRANSMISSION

Single dry plate clutch, open propeller shaft with needle-bearing universal joints, hypoid semi-floating final drive, ratio: 3.73: 1 (3.41: 1 available on 'R' Type; 3.07: 1 on the *Continental*).

SUSPENSION

Front: Coil spring independent with hydraulic shock dampers.
Rear: Semi-elliptic with hydraulic shock dampers controllable from lever on steering wheel.

BRAKES

Internal expanding drum, servo assisted, hydraulic front, mechanical rear.

CHASSIS LUBRICATION

Complete centralised system fed from reservoir on dash by foot-operated pump.

STEERING

Cam and roller.

WHEELS

16″ carrying 6–50 x 16 tyres.

PRINCIPAL DIMENSIONS

Wheelbase: 10′ 0″
Front Track: 4′ 8½″
Rear Track: 4′ 10½″
Turning Circle: 41′ 0″

NUMBER PRODUCED

Mk. VI — 5,201
'R' Type — 2,528 of which 208 were *Continentals*

CHASSIS NUMBERS

Mk. VI

B2-254AK, B1-247AJ	1946-7	B2-500NZ, B1-501NY	1951-2
B2-400BM, B1-401BG	1947	B2-300PV, B1-301PU	1952
B2-500CF, B1-501CD	1947-8	*'R'-Type*	
B2-500DA, B1-501DZ	1948-9	B2-120RT, B1-121RS	1952
B2-500EY, B1-501EW	1949	B2-500SR, B1-501SP	1952-3
B2-500FV, B1-601FU	1949-50	B1-401TO, B2-600TN	1953
B1-401GT	1950	B1-251UL, B2-250UM	1953-4
B2-250HR, B1-251HP	1950	B2-300WH, B1-301WG	1954
B2-250JO, B1-251JN	1950-1	B2-140XF	1954
B2-200KM, B1-201KL	1951	B1--331YA, B2-330YD	1954
B2-400LJ, B1-401LM	1951	B1-251ZX, B2-250ZY	1954-5
B2-400MD, B1-401MB	1951		

With the exception of the *Continentals*, all series starting with 1 use only odd numbers, while those starting with 2 use only evens. Number 13 not used. 'L' before chassis letters indicates a left-hand drive car.

'R'-type Continental

BC1-26A	1952
BC1-25B	1952-3
BC1-78C	1953-4
BC1-74D	1954-5
BC1-9E	1955

116. 1952 *Bentley* Continental two door Saloon by H.J. Mulliner.

117. Three variations of H.J. Mulliner's 'Lightweight' theme.

118. Two door Drophead Coupé.

119. Four door Sports Saloon.

The Silver Wraith

The *Silver Wraith* was a model designed before the war but not introduced until 1947 and was basically a *Wraith* with revised valve layout (F-head, as previously mentioned in reference to the *Mk. VI* Bentley), and other modifications to the 4,257 c.c. 29.4 h.p. engine. The wheelbase was shortened from 11 feet 4 inches to 10 feet 7 inches and other changes to the chassis included bolt-on disc wheels (previously these were of the centre-lock wire type) and modified front suspension.

Described in the motoring Press as the best Rolls-Royce ever, the *Silver Wraith* even after twenty years of use, is a sheer delight to drive. A well-kept *Silver Wraith* will perform smoothly and silently at all speeds to a maximum in the region of 90 m.p.h. No modern car can match its refinement.

The *Silver Wraith* chassis was never fitted with standard steel coachwork, the customer instead chose from a magnificent selection offered by the various coachbuilders still in existence at that time. The standard specification of these superbly luxurious carriages could, of course, be altered to suit the tastes of individual clients.

Over the years the *Silver Wraith* underwent many changes, the final version having the 4.9-litre twin-carburettor engine, an automatic gearbox and power-assisted steering in common with the *Silver Cloud*. In 1951 the 4,566 c.c. 'big-bore' engine replaced the 4,257 c.c. version. At the same time the long wheelbase *Silver Wraith* was introduced as an option to the short wheelbase version to facilitate the fitting of coachwork with even roomier rear compartments and longer luggage boots. The additional six inches of wheelbase made these cars an admirable substitute for those whose status did not allow them to aspire to *Phantom IV* ownership (all but Royalty and Heads of State were refused the *Phantom IV*). The long wheelbase model became so popular with coachbuilders and clients that by 1953 all efforts were concentrated upon it, the short version being dropped from the range.

ROLLS-ROYCE SILVER WRAITH IN PRODUCTION 1946-1958

ENGINE

Six cylinders in line. *1946* Bore $3\frac{1}{2}$ inches, stroke $4\frac{1}{2}$ inches, 4,257 c.c. 29.4 h.p. (R.A.C. rating). *1951* Bore $3\frac{5}{8}$ inches, stroke $4\frac{1}{2}$ inches, 4,566 c.c. 31.5 h.p. (R.A.C. rating). *1956* Bore $3\frac{3}{4}$ inches, stroke $4\frac{1}{2}$ inches, 4,887 c.c. 33.7 h.p. (R.A.C. rating). Overhead inlet, side exhaust valves, aluminium cylinder head, single Stromberg or Zenith carburettor, (Twin S.U.'s from 1956) twin S.U. fuel pumps.

120. A *Silver Wraith*

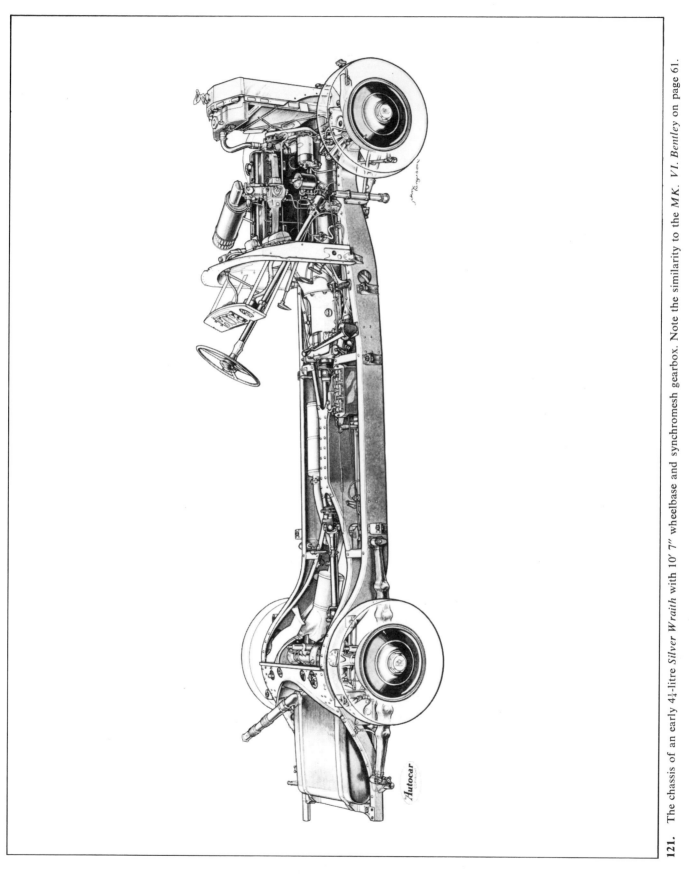

121. The chassis of an early 4¼-litre *Silver Wraith* with 10′ 7″ wheelbase and synchromesh gearbox. Note the similarity to the *MK. VI. Bentley* on page 61.

122 1947 *Silver Wraith* Sports Saloon by James Young.
123 1949 *Silver Wraith* Saloon by James Young.

124. H.J. Mulliner's beautifully proportioned Sports Saloon with division introduced in 1948.
125. 1949 *Silver Wraith* Sedanca-de-Ville by H.J.Mulliner.

126. *Above left* A masterpiece in walnut veneer behind the division in James Young's Touring Limousine.
127. *Above right* The 1951 *Silver Wraith* Saloon with coachwork by James Young owned by Miss Joan Hammond CBE of Airey's Inlet.

128. 1951 Rolls-Royce *Silver Wraith* four door six-light Saloon with coachwork by Freestone & Webb Ltd.

GEARBOX

Four speed and reverse, synchromesh on second, third and top gears, side control, (column control on L.H. drive cars).

Ratios: *1st,* 2.98: 1, *2nd,* 2.1: 1, *3rd,* 1.34: 1, *Top,* 1: 1. Rolls-Royce automatic gearbox available from 1952, made standard in 1955.

Ratios: *1st,* 3.82: 1, *2nd,* 2.63: 1, *3rd,* 1.45: 1, *Top,* 1: 1.

TRANSMISSION

Single dry plate clutch, divided propeller shaft, hypoid final drive with semi-floating half-shafts, ratio 11: 41, 8: 34 from 1955, 9: 35 from 1956.

SUSPENSION

Front: Coil spring independent with hydraulic shock dampers.

Rear: Semi-elliptic with hydraulic shock dampers, controllable from lever on steering wheel.

BRAKES

Internal expanding drum, servo-assisted, hydraulic front, mechanical rear.

CHASSIS LUBRICATION

Complete centralised system fed from reservoir on dash by foot-operated pump.

STEERING

Cam and roller, power assisted steering available from 1956.

WHEELS

17″ carrying 6.50 x 17 tyres, long wheelbase cars 16″ with 7.50 x 16 tyres.

PRINCIPAL DIMENSIONS

Wheelbase: 10′ 7″ (long wheelbase 11′ 1″)
Front Track: 4′ 10″ (long wheelbase 4′ 10″)
Rear Track: 5′ 0″ (long wheelbase 5′ 4″)
Turning Circle: 43′ 5″ (long wheelbase 45′ 5″)

NUMBERS PRODUCED

1,783 of which 639 were long wheelbase cars.

CHASSIS NUMBERS

WTA1-85, WVA1-81,		WHD1-101	1950
WYA1-87	1946-7	WLE1-35, WME1-96	1950-1
WZB1-65, WAB1-65,		WOF1-76	1951
WCB1-73	1947-8	WSG1-76	1951-2
WDC1-101, WFC1-101,		WVH1-116	1952
WGC1-101	1948-50		

Long wheelbase

ALW1-51	1951	ELW1-101	1955-6
BLW1-101	1952-3	FLW1-101	1956-7
CLW1-43	1953-4	GLW1-26	1957
DLW1-166	1954-5	HLW1-52	1958

'L' before letters indicates left- hand drive car. Number 13 not used.

129. In 1951 H.J. Mulliner redesigned their *Silver Wraith* style. The result is a most strikingly beautiful car.

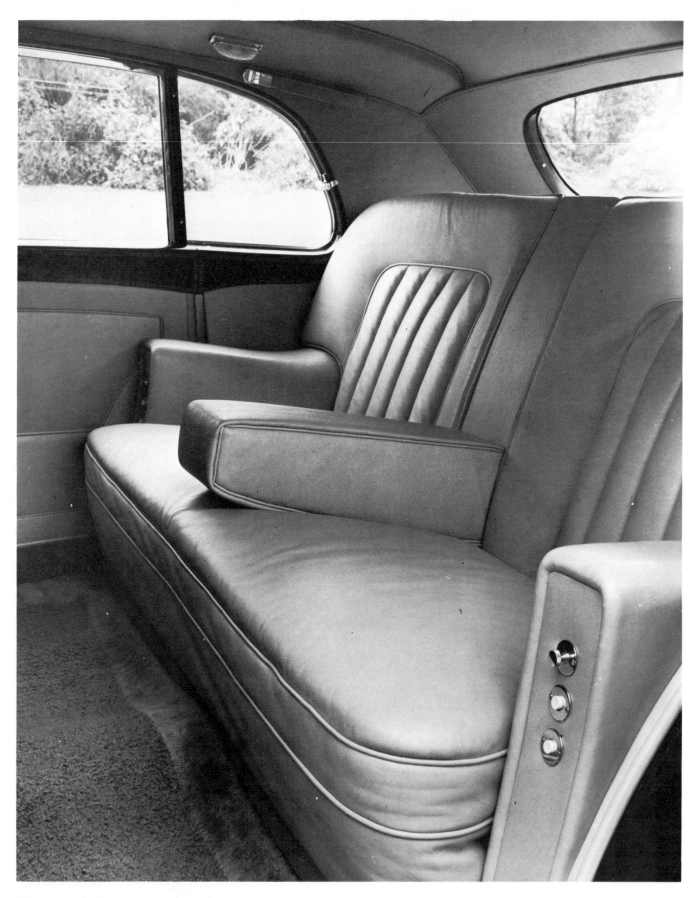

130. The luxurious rear-compartment of the H.J. Mulliner Touring Limousine.

131. The beautifully veneered instrument panel.
132. Even the boot appears luxurious!

133. 1951 *Silver Wraith* Saloon by James Young. Note the built-in headlights.
134. A *Silver Wraith* line-up in the USA.

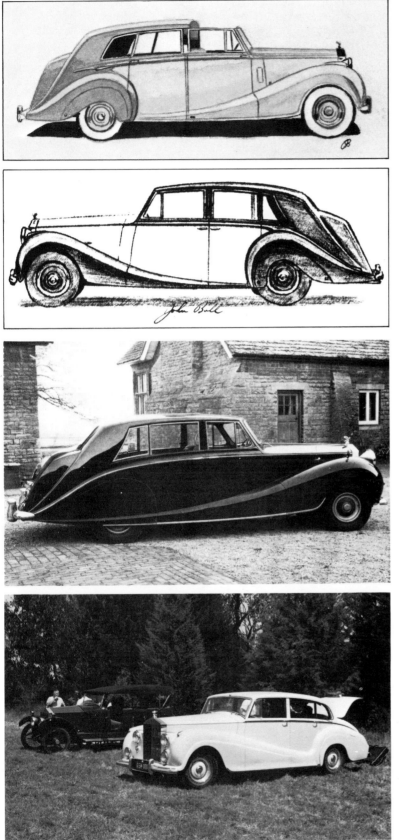

135. 1952 *Silver Wraith* Sedanca-de-Ville by Franay. Price £8,000.

136. 1950 Hooper Touring Limousine on Rolls-Royce *Silver Wraith* chassis.

137. 1954 *Silver Wraith* Sports Saloon by Hooper.

138. 1953 *Silver Wraith* Touring Limousine by Park Ward, chassis no. BLW 78, owned by Mrs Nancy Rolls of Victoria, Australia. Also shown is its noble ancestor the 20 h.p.

139.

140. 1948 *Silver Wraith* Hooper Touring Limousine.

141. 1957 *Silver Wraith* Hooper Touring Limousine.

142. 1957 *Silver Wraith* seven passenger Limousine by Hooper.

143. A Park Ward advertisement illustrating their spacious saloon coachwork introduced in 1950. Reprinted from 'Motor', 27 September 1950.

144. 1948 *Silver Wraith* seven passenger Limousine by Park Ward.

145. 1948 *Silver Wraith* Sports Saloon by Park Ward.

146. An early *Silver Wraith* instrument layout.

147. 1953 *Silver Wraith* Touring Limousine by H.J. Mulliner.

148. 1957 *Silver Wraith* Park Ward Saloon.

149. *Right* Rolls-Royce right-hand gear-change lever. The knob is pressed down to select reverse.

150. *Below* 1957 Silver Wraith price list.

ROLLS-ROYCE
SILVER WRAITH

		Basic Price	Purchase Tax	Total Price
CHASSIS		£2,695	£674 8 6	£3,369 8 6
TOURING SALOON	(Coachwork by Park Ward & Co. Ltd.)	£5,270	£2,636 7 0	£7,906 7 0
SEVEN PASSENGER LIMOUSINE	(Coachwork by Park Ward & Co. Ltd.)	£5,570	£2,786 7 0	£8,356 7 0
TOURING LIMOUSINE	(Coachwork by Hooper & Co. Ltd.)	£5,395	£2,698 17 0	£8,093 17 0
SEVEN PASSENGER LIMOUSINE	(Coachwork by Hooper & Co. Ltd.)	£5,570	£2,786 7 0	£8,356 7 0
TOURING LIMOUSINE	(Coachwork by H. J. Mulliner & Co. Ltd.)	£5,380	£2,691 7 0	£8,071 7 0
FOUR DOOR SALOON	(Coachwork by James Young Ltd.)	£5,445	£2,723 17 0	£8,168 17 0

ROLLS-ROYCE LTD   14-15 CONDUIT STREET   LONDON W.I
Telephone: Mayfair 6201   Telegrams: "Railhead Piccy, London"   Works: Crewe, Cheshire

The specification and prices are subject to alteration without notice.

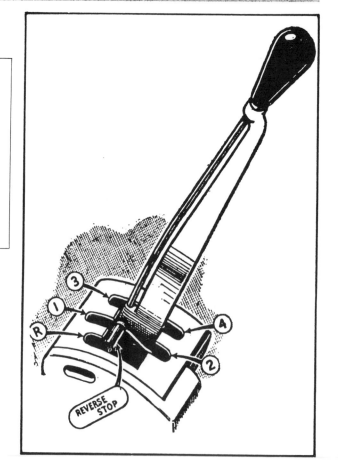

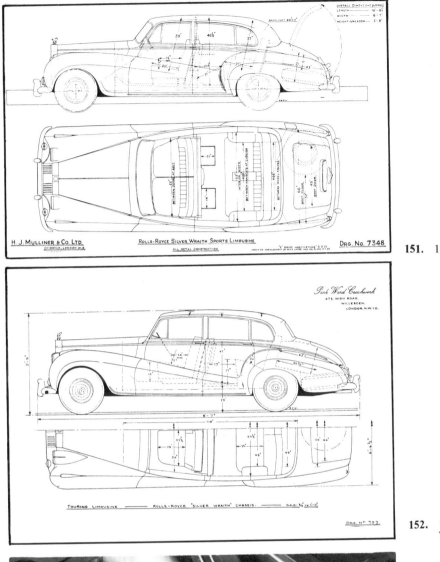

151. 1958 *Silver Wraith.*

152. 1957 *Silver Wraith* Touring Limousine by Park Ward.

153. *Silver Wraith* chassis construction showing massive cruciform member.

154. *Silver Wraith* Touring Limousine by Freestone & Webb.
155. 1955 Long wheelbase *Silver Wraith* Drophead Coupé by Park Ward.

156. *Above* 1958 Rolls-Royce seven passenger Limousine. This was James Young's final *Silver Wraith* body style. Note the similarity between this design and that of the same company's *Phantom V* designs of the following year.

157. Hooper Cabriolet-de-Ville supplied to the Australian Department of Supply in 1959. Two such cars were supplied and were finished in black and claret.

158. The opulent interior of a 1958 Limousine by James Young. The doors below the picnic tables are folding carpeted footrests.

159. 1958 *Silver Wraith* Touring Limousine by Hooper.
160. 1959 *Silver Wraith* seven passenger Limousine by Park Ward.

The 'Royal Rolls'

In 1950 the company introduced a special car indeed. The *Phantom IV*, of which only eighteen were built, is likely to remain the most exclusive Rolls ever; available to Royalty and Heads of State only, these cars were originally designed by request of Their Royal Highnesses Princess Elizabeth (now Queen Elizabeth II) and the Duke of Edinburgh. The *Silver Wraith* chassis was lengthened by 18 inches and fitted with a refined B80 straight-eight engine, which meant that the car was unusually long for the 'fifties. However, size is of small consequence for a processional carriage, and the inevitably-long bonnet balanced the car's proportions rather admirably. The only other Rolls-Royce-built car to be fitted with the straight-eight was a modified *Mk. V* Bentley known by the initials 'SC', which was said to have stood for 'Scalded Cat'. The bore and stroke of the straight-eight were, of course, identical to the six, the two extra cylinders giving a capacity of 5,675 c.c. Not by any means a large 'eight', but sufficient to give these very large cars a top speed of around 100 m.p.h.

LIST OF ROLLS-ROYCE PHANTOM IV CARS

CHASSIS NO.
4 AF 2   Mulliner Special Limousine—Painted Valentine Green. Delivered to Their Royal Highnesses The Duke of Edinburgh and the Princess Elizabeth on 6 July 1950.
4 AF 4   Open Delivery Wagon—Owned and used by Rolls-Royce.
4 AF 6   Mulliner Two-Door Drophead 4-Passenger Coupé. Colour—Light Metallic Blue—White Leather. Delivered on 3 December 1951 to H.I.M. The Shahinshah of Iran.
4 AF 8   Mulliner Saloon—Painted Royal Blue and Orange Biscuit. Delivered on 29 March 1950 to the Ruler of Kuwait.
4 AF 10 Delivered to the Duke of Gloucester.

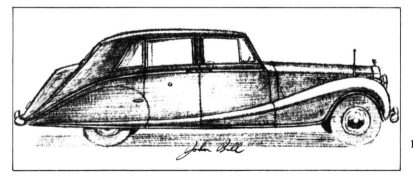

161. Hooper Limousine built in 1953 for H.H. the late Prince Abdullilah of Iraq on Rolls-Royce *Phantom IV* chassis.

162. Rolls-Royce *Phantom IV* Sedanca-de-Ville by Hooper owned by Thomas Barratt in the USA. This car was originally built for H.H. The Aga Khan. Chassis No. 4AF 20.

4 AF 12   Hooper 7-Passenger Limousine—Painted Deep Blue. Delivered on 20 November 1953 to H.R.H. The Duchess of Kent (now Princess Marina).

4 AF 14   Mulliner 5-Passenger Limousine—Armour Plate to rear. Delivered on 13 June 1952 to H.E. Generalissimo Franco.

4 AF 16   Mulliner 7-Passenger Limousine—Armour Plate to rear. Ordered 18 October 1948 and delivered on 4 July 1952. Colour—Black. Price £8,580. Delivered to H.E. Generalissimo Franco.

4 AF 18   Mulliner 5-Passenger Folding Head Cabriolet—Painted Black. Green Leather. Rear Compartment Armour Plated.
Ordered 18 October 1948 and delivered on 28 March 1952 to H.E. Generalissimo Franco.

4 AF 20   Hooper Special Sedanca-De-Ville—Ordered 25 April 1950 and delivered on 4 June 1952 to H.H. Prince Aga Khan. Paintwork—Two shades of Green. Upholstery—Red leather.

4 AF 22   Coachbuilder—Franay of France. Delivered to H.R.H. Prince Talal al Saoud Ryal, Saudi Arabia.

4 BP 1   Hooper Touring Limousine—Delivered to H.M. King Feisal II.

4 BP 3   Hooper Touring Limousine—Delivered on 11 October 1952 to H.R.H. Prince Regent of Iraq.

4 BP 5   Hooper Landaulette—Paintwork—Claret and Black. Built especially for the Coronation of Queen Elizabeth.

4 BP 7   Mulliner 7-Passenger Limousine—Paintwork—Black. Delivered on 29 March 1950 to the Ruler of Kuwait.

4 CS 2   Mulliner 6-Light Saloon—Colour—Light Green and Opaline Green. Delivered on 1 February 1955 to H.H. The Ruler of Kuwait, H.H. Shaikh Sin Abdulla al Salim al Subak.

4 CS 4   Mulliner 4-Light Saloon—Paint—Golden Beige. Delivered on 9 February 1955. Customer—H.H. The Ruler of Kuwait, H.H. Shaikh Sin Abdulla al Salim al Subak.

4 CS 6   Hooper Limousine—Colour—Black. Delivered on 29 December 1955 to H.I.M. The Shah of Persia.

1952 ROLLS-ROYCE PHANTOM IV-CHASSIS NO. 4AF 20

Coachbuilder—Hooper & Company
Ordered by His Highness the Aga Khan III
Body type—Sedanca de Ville
His Highness Aga Khan III

The Aga Khan earned the reputation over the means of being most meticulous about the coachwork on the chassis of his choice. It is interesting to note the fine attention to detail given this particular chassis by the Aga Khan. It would also be difficult to find another luxury to install in this fine example of the ultimate in craftmanship. ship.

Present Ownership

There is an unconfirmed report that by agreement with Rolls-Royce at the time of original purchase it was agreed that the Aga Khan would never re-sell the *Phantom IV* but if he ever desired to dispose of it he must turn it back to the Rolls-Royce Factory. When he died in 1957 his estate acquired title to the *Phantom IV* and his wife subsequently sold the Rolls-Royce to a third party. His death effectively circumvented the agreement with Rolls-Royce and as a result we all have the privilege of admiring this beautiful automobile.

In 1961 Mr. Heiss of the Mayfair-Lennox Hotel in St. Louis, Missouri acquired the *Phantom IV* for the explicit purpose of transporting dignitaries from the Airport and Railway Depot to his hotel. Luggage carrying capacity of the *Phantom IV* proved inadequate which necessitated sale of the car.

In November 1962 the *Phantom IV* was acquired by Mr. and Mrs. Elwood L. Hansen of Hillsborough, California, and is now owned by Mr Thomas Barratt in the United States.
Phantom IV Rolls-Royce 4 AF 20

PURCHASE ORDER

written by Rolls-Royce
Purchaser—Franco-Britiannic Auto's SA
                    25 Rue Paul Vaillant Couturier
                    Levallois-Perret, Seine Office
                    27 Avenue Kleber, Paris XVI
Ordered 25 April 1950. Shipped on 6 April 1952 on S/S Maidstone, Folkestone—Bologne.
Model—Phantom IV
Engine—P 10 A

Customer—H.H. Prince Aga Khan
            Villa Yakimour
            Le Cannet, Cannes AM

Type of Body—Special Sedanca De Ville

Paintwork—Two shades of Green

Upholstery—Red Leather UM 3086, Red Headlining and Carpet
Red Mohair Rug to rear floor.

Terms—22½% and 15% Body

Remarks—Speedo in KMS, Two R-100 Headlamps, Two foglamps, Continental Chassis Plate, U.S. Type Bumpers, 8 x 17 Tyres Am 211, No Radio.

Details—Nearside doors fitted with Private Locks. All door windows electrically operated and controlled by self-cancelling switches let flush into wood panels of doors. All window mechanisms fitted with manually operated window winding device.

Deflecting panels to rear end of main door windows and to forward ends of front door windows operated by controls on the garnish rails. Quarter windows fixed with a shutter on the inside and made to slide forward and partially obscure the quarter windows. Mirror fitted on inside face of shutter.

Loose covers to the front and rear compartment cushions and squabs in red cloth piped leather. Electrically operated blind to rear window. Folding arm rest to centre of rear seat with shallow leather lined tray fitted with silver back comb, cloth brush, two cut glass jars with silver tops and solid silver compact—Compact and Silver tops to be engraved with H.H. Aga Khan crest. Top of armrest to hinge up as lid with hinged mirror.

Polished wood cabinet on back of division between occasional seats, automatically illuminated with opening of cabinet door.

Fitted with two thermos flasks, two sandwich boxes, four plates and one nest of four silver beakers with gilt interior.

Two small tables above folding seats.

Two-way switches for the division window on either side of the rear seat on the quarters.

Two wing mirrors.

Crests.

Locks to Bonnet AM 278 7-23-51.

Ash trays and lighters to front and rear.

Hand operated microphone from rear compartment to driver.

ROLLS-ROYCE PHANTOM IV
IN PRODUCTION 1950-1956

ENGINE

Eight cylinders in line, firing order 16258374. Bore 3¼ inches, stroke 4½ inches, 5,675 c.c., 40 h.p. (R.A.C. rating). Overhead inlet, side exhaust valves, aluminium cylinder head, single Stromberg carburettor, four fuel pumps.

GEARBOX

Four speed and reverse, synchromesh on second, third and top gears, right-hand control.

Rolls-Royce automatic gearbox on later cars.

Ratios: *1st*, 3: 1, *2nd*, 2.01: 1, *3rd*, 1.35: 1, *Top*, 1: 1.

TRANSMISSION

Single dry plate clutch, universal joints on propeller shaft fitted with needle roller-bearings, hypoid semi-floating final drive, ratio 4.25: 1.

SUSPENSION

Front: Coil spring independent with hydraulic shock dampers.

Rear: Semi-elliptic with hydraulic shock dampers controlled from lever on steering wheel.

BRAKES

Internal expanding drum, servo assisted, hydraulic front, mechanical rear.

CHASSIS LUBRICATION

Complete centralised system fed from reservoir on dash by foot operated pump.

STEERING

Cam and roller.

WHEELS

17″ carrying 7.00 x 17 tyres.

PRINCIPAL DIMENSIONS

Wheelbase: 12′ 1″

Front Track: 4′ 10½″

Rear Track: 5′ 3″

NUMBER PRODUCED

18.

The Silver Dawn

The standard steel saloon coachwork was confined to the Bentley chassis until 1949 when a new Rolls-Royce was introduced for the export market. The new model was basically a *Mk. VI* Bentley with the *Silver Wraith* engine (one carburettor) and a new design of Rolls-Royce radiator incorporating twenty-two fixed shutters, (previously there had only been fourteen, thermostatically controlled according to water temperature). The steel bodywork differed only in the shape of the bonnet and the layout of the instrument panel. By 1953 this car was available on the home market, with 4½-litre engine, automatic transmission and big boot coachwork as fitted to the 'R' type Bentley. Although the great majority of the 760 *Silver Dawns* sported the standard bodies a few had specialised coachwork.

163. Reprinted from 1953 catalogue.

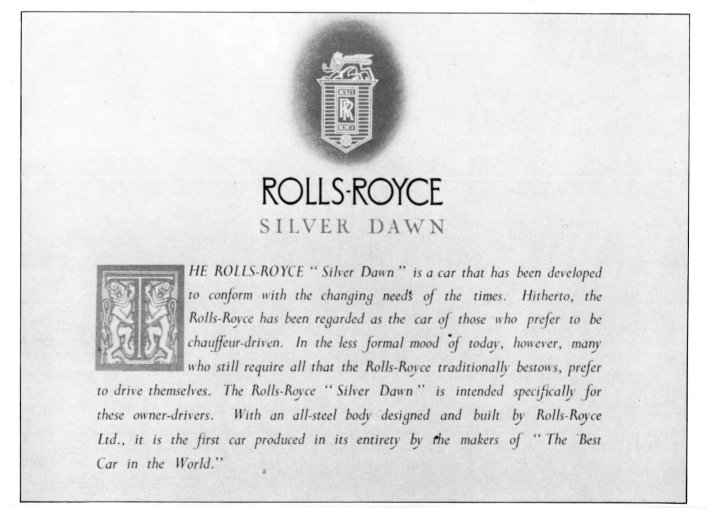

ROLLS-ROYCE

SILVER DAWN

HE ROLLS-ROYCE " Silver Dawn " is a car that has been developed to conform with the changing needs of the times. Hitherto, the Rolls-Royce has been regarded as the car of those who prefer to be chauffeur-driven. In the less formal mood of today, however, many who still require all that the Rolls-Royce traditionally bestows, prefer to drive themselves. The Rolls-Royce " Silver Dawn " is intended specifically for these owner-drivers. With an all-steel body designed and built by Rolls-Royce Ltd., it is the first car produced in its entirety by the makers of " The Best Car in the World."

164. *Silver Dawn* standard steel Saloon. This model with a short luggage boot was built for export only.

165. *Silver Dawn* Saloon. Reprinted from catalogue.

166. 167. *Silver Dawn* instrument panel showing (a) left-hand steering with column gear change (b) right-hand steering with conventional gear lever.

(b)

168. 1954 *Silver Dawn* showing long boot.

CHASSIS NUMBERS		SKE2-50, SLE1-51	1952-3
SBA2-138, SCA1-63	1949-51	SMF2-76, SNF1-125	1953-4
SDB2-140	1951	SOG2-100, SPG1-101	1954
SFC2-160	1951-2	SRH2-100, STH1-101	1954
SHD2-60	1952	SUJ2-130, SVJ1-133	1954-5

Series starting with 1 use only odd numbers while those starting with 2 use only evens. Number 13 not used. 'L' before letters indicates left-hand drive car.

Number of cars produced, 706.

169. 1953 *Silver Dawn* Saloon by James Young.
170. 1954 *Silver Dawn* Saloon by James Young.

ROLLS-ROYCE · SILVER DAWN · ABRIDGED SPECIFICATION

COACHWORK. The all-steel body is built to be as light as possible, consistent with strength and rigidity and is specially treated to avoid "drumming." There are two separate sliding front seats, while the back seat accommodates three passengers. All seats are upholstered in leather in "pleated and bolster" style, and folding tables are fitted in the backs of the front seats. Footrests are also provided.

HEATER. The heater is situated under the front seat and the air is circulated to both front and rear compartments by means of an electric fan.

DE-MISTER AND DE-FROSTER. Fresh air is taken in at the front of the car and after being heated by the radiator matrix is fed through the windscreen ducts, the volume being augmented by a motor-driven fan.

RADIO. A six-valve medium and long wave, or short and medium wave radio is fitted, with an outside aerial. Push-button control on instrument panel.

ENGINE. Six cylinders with overhead inlet and side exhaust valves. Bore $3\frac{5}{8}$ in. (92 mm.), stroke $4\frac{1}{2}$ in. (114 mm.), capacity 4,566 c.c.

CARBURETTER. Down-draught aero type, with automatic mixture control for all conditions including cold starting.

IGNITION. By battery and coil.

COOLING SYSTEM. By fan and centrifugal pump. Temperature thermostatically controlled. Temperature indicator on instrument panel.

CLUTCH. Single dry-plate type, with compensating linkage between pedal and clutch to allow freedom of engine-movement.

GEARBOX. Four speed and reverse, synchromesh on 2nd, 3rd and 4th, which is direct drive. Control lever on left-hand steering column. Alternatively, right-hand steering with gear lever is conventional position on right of driver's seat.

SUSPENSION. Front—Independent, helical springs with hydraulic dampers. Rear—Semi-elliptic springs with hydraulic dampers, controllable by a lever on the steering column.

STEERING. Left-hand or right-hand steering is fitted as required.

BRAKES. Mechanical at rear, hydraulic at front. Operation assisted by mechanical servo mounted on side of gearbox. Handbrake supplements operation of rear brakes.

CHASSIS LUBRICATION. Centralised system supplied by reservoir and pedal-operated pump mounted on dash panel. System includes front and rear suspension.

PETROL SUPPLY. 18 gallons. Twin electric pumps. Fuel gauge on instrument panel, and warning light which operates when fuel is low.

JACKING SYSTEM. Side jacking system, the jack operating on a slide extending under the body sill, at about the centre of the chassis.

TYRES. 6.50 in. on 16 in. disc wheels.

DIMENSIONS. Wheelbase 10ft., front track 4 ft. $8\frac{1}{2}$ ins., turning circle 42 ft. 6 in.

171. Reprinted from catalogue.
172. *Below* 1952 *Silver Dawn* Drophead Coupé by Park Ward.
173. *Right* 1952 *Silver Dawn* Drophead Coupé.

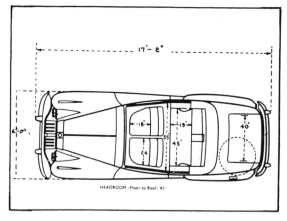

A New Rolls-Royce Image

In 1955 a new model was introduced which was said to have altered the entire Rolls-Royce image; it was in fact the most radically new Rolls ever and with its long, streamlined bodywork it was an instant hit in the United States as well as in Britain. Previously sales in the U.S. were slow and the new car, known as the *Silver Cloud*, and its Bentley equivalent, called the '*S*' series, revived the American sales to the extent that it became the biggest Rolls-Royce export market.

The Rolls-Royce and Bentley versions of the car differed only in the radiator shells and identification markings. The engine used was the final development of the six-cylinder 'F'-head engine, introduced in 1954 for the Bentley *Continental*. Like the Bentley, the *Silver Cloud* was fitted with twin carburettors (for the first time in a production Rolls-Royce). The resultant slight forfeiture of flexibility was of small consequence to the owners as automatic transmission was fitted as standard equipment.

Features prominent for decades in the specifications of Rolls-Royce cars were still evident in the *Silver Cloud*. The lever on the steering wheel for the adjustable rear shock dampers was replaced by an electric two-position switch on the steering column. A second hydraulic braking circuit operating on the front brake drums and the mechanical system operating on the rear. That admirable but not entirely infallible feature of the marque, the centralised or 'one-shot' chassis lubrication system was retained at first, to be abandoned in 1959 in favour of twenty-one grease points requiring attention only every 12,000 miles. Many of the new features, including the 4,887 c.c. engine, were also included in the specification of the *Silver Wraith* cars from 1956. The *Silver Cloud* was a very modern car. The work put into its design was well rewarded by a flood of orders from every corner of the world where the name Rolls-Royce is known and respected as a synonym for 'the best money can buy'. Never before had so many orders come from the United States, and in Hollywood the *Silver Cloud* became almost commonplace. The Company's advertising policy in the U.S. changed under Mr David Ogilvy from the subtle and perhaps arrogant style well-known in Britain to something rather more imaginative. Captions such as 'At 60 m.p.h. the loudest noise in the new Rolls-Royce comes from the electric clock' or 'The new Rolls-Royce is intended to be owner-driven, no chauffeur required' were used. The latter was aimed at emphasising that the *Silver Cloud* was completely correct at all times, and not only when in the hands of a professional chauffeur (an opinion prevalent in the United States). This caption was usually accompanied by a colour picture depicting a typical American family in a new Rolls passing along an equally typical American Turnpike.

174. *Silver Cloud* chassis.

175. A New Rolls-Royce Image, The *Silver Cloud* and *Bentley 'S'* series pose together.

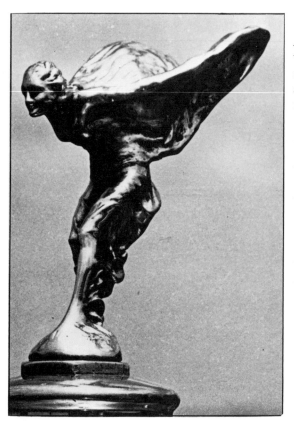

176. New version of the standing 'Spirit of Ecstasy' as used on the *Silver Cloud*.

The radiator shell of the *Silver Cloud* was similar to that of the *Dawn,* with twenty-two fixed slats, but the 'Spirit of Ecstasy' mascot was changed to a new five-inch version of Charles Sykes' original standing lady. The Bentley winged 'B' mascot was modernised by abandoning the dummy filler cap upon which this was previously mounted.

The interiors of the new cars set a very high standard. They were furnished, as in the *Silver Dawn,* in the finest coachbuilding tradition using such materials as the Circassion Walnut Veneers, leather upholstery, West of England cloth headlining and deep pile Wilton carpets. The high-set front seat offered a particularly commanding view of the road ahead over the not-too-long tapering bonnet, while passengers riding in the rear compartment did so in luxury and seclusion. As was usual, standard equipment included hot and cold air ventilation, full demisting (including electrically heated rear window), cigar lighters front and rear, electric clock, press-button radio, electrically operated petrol-filler flap and electrically actuated adjustable rear dampers. As in previous models, vanity mirrors which could be illuminated for use at night and folding picnic tables were provided to enhance the luxury of the rear compartment.

THE SILVER CLOUD CHASSIS

The vast improvements incorporated in the mechanics of the *Silver Cloud* warrant a detailed examination. The 4,887 c.c. six cylinder engine represented the final form of that which was introduced in 1922 for the 20 h.p. model and, as throughout the thirty-seven years of its development it still retained the original centre-to-centre bore dimensions and $4\frac{1}{2}$ inches stroke.

The drive was taken via the automatic gearbox and ball-and-trunnion sliding joint by a divided propeller shaft to the hypoid bevel final drive, which incorporated four-star differential and semi-floating half-shafts.

The cam and roller steering with transverse drag link and three piece track linkage was available with hydraulic power assistance as an optional extra from 1957. This particularly desirable refinement enabled the big car to steer effortlessly and accurately throughout the speed range without robbing the driver of 'feel'.

Modifications to the i.f.s. enabled greater wheel movements, and the dampers had larger, horizontally-mounted cylinders. The rear springs were still semi-elliptic.

The fade-free Girling Autostatic drum brakes, provided with three independent braking circuits, were still powered by the classic Rolls-Royce transmission-driven mechanical servo unit which gave assistance in direct proportion to pedal pressure.

The chassis frame was an immensely strong and rigid structure, with two box-section side members and cruciform cross members pierced to take the drive shaft. In fact the new chassis represented a full 50 per cent increase in torsional rigidity over that of the *Silver Dawn.*

CHASSIS NUMBERS

Silver Cloud I

SWA2-250, SXA1-125	1955-6	SFE1-501, SGE2-500	1957-8
SYB2-250, SZB1-251	1956	SHF1-249, SJF2-250	1958-9

SBC2-150, SCC1-151	1956-7	SKG1-125, SLG2-126	1959
SDD2-450, SED1-451	1957-8	SMH1-265, SNH2-262	1959
		Total—2,238 cars	

Long Wheelbase Silver Cloud I

ALC1-26	CLC1-47
BLC1-51	Total—121 cars

Bentley S1

B2AN-B500AN, B1AP-B501AP	B2EG-B650EG, B1EK-B651EK	
1955-6	1957-8	
B2BA-B250BA, B1BC-B251BC	B2FA-B650FA, B1FD-B651FD	
1956	1957-9	
B2CK-B500CK, B1CM-B501CM	B1GD-B125GD, B2GC-B126GC	
1956	1959	
B2DB-B350DB, B1DE-B351DE	B1HB-B45HB, B2HA-B50HA	
1956-7	1959	
	Total—3,072 cars	

Long Wheelbase S1

ALB1-36	1959
Total—35 cars	

Continental S1

BC1AF-BC102AF	1955	BC1EL-BC51EL	1957-8
BC1BG-BC101BG	1955-6	BC1FM-BC51FM	1958
BC1CH-BC51CH	1957	BC1GN-BC31GN	1958
BC1DJ-BC51DJ	1957	Total—431 cars	

With the exception of the long wheelbase and *Continental* series, all series starting with 1 use odd numbers only while those starting with 2 use evens only. The number 13 was not used. 'L' before chassis letters indicates left-hand drive car.

Silver Cloud Performance Figures:
'Autocar' May 1958.
Acceleration:

From rest to 30 mph through gears						4.1 secs
,,	,,	,, 50 mph	,,	,,		9.4 secs
,,	,,	,, 60 mph	,,	,,		13.0 secs
,,	,,	,, 70 mph	,,	,,		18.4 secs
,,	,,	,, 80 mph	,,	,,		25.0 secs
,,	,,	,, 90 mph	,,	,,		34.1 secs
,,	,,	,,100 mph	,,	,,		50.6 secs

Maximum speeds in gears:
Top: 106 mph
3rd: 63 mph
2nd: 34 mph
1st: 24 mph
Fuel consumption: 12 m.p.g.

The coachwork of the Rolls-Royce 'Silver Cloud' does not slavishly follow the dictates of fashion; a five-seater saloon with room for six when required, it is a luxurious yet practical motor car. The gently sloping bonnet, curved windscreen, and large rear window mean improved visibility, while the new car is lower with no reduction of head room.

The independent heating and demisting systems provide complete control over the temperature and speed of entry of fresh air into the car, so obviating the necessity of opening windows which causes wind roar when travelling fast.

177. Extract from the catalogue for the *Silver Cloud*.
178. *Silver Cloud* and *Bentley 'S'* series specification from 1956 Rolls-Royce and Bentley catalogue. These cars were in production from 1955 to 1959.

ENGINE

Six cylinders Bore and Stroke 3¾ × 4½ in. (95 × 114 mm.) 4887 cc. Overhead inlet valves through push rods and rockers. Side exhaust valves. Compression ratio 6·6 : 1. Firing order 142635. Piston area 66·26 sq. in. Crankshaft nitrided, with integral balance weights. Seven main bearings. Aluminium pistons. 3 compression and 1 scraper ring. Top ring chromium plated. Two S.U. carburettors of new diaphragm type.

TRANSMISSION

Four-speed automatic transmission in unit with engine. Divided propeller shaft. Hypoid bevel final drive with four-star differential and semi-floating half shafts.
Rear axle 3·42 to 1.
Overall transmission ratios—
1st 13·06 to 1, 2nd 9·00 to 1, 3rd 4·96 to 1, 4th 3·42 to 1, Reverse 14·72 to 1.

CHASSIS

Closed box section frame of welded steel construction with cruciform centre bracing pierced for propeller shaft and forming a very stiff structure. Steel front pan carrying the suspension and steering.

SUSPENSION

Independent front suspension by wishbones of unequal length, with coil springs. Rolls-Royce opposed piston hydraulic dampers and torsional anti-roll bar. Rear suspension by half-elliptic springs with rubber-bushed shackles and electrically controlled piston-type dampers. "Z"-type anti-roll bar.

STEERING

Cam and roller connected by transverse link to a three-piece track linkage.

WHEELS AND TYRES

15 in. steel disc wheels on five studs, carrying 8·20 in. broad base tyres.

BRAKES

Servo unit assisted brakes, with hydraulic operation at the front. Combined hydraulic and mechanical operation at the rear. Pull and twist handbrake operating on rear wheels. Cast-iron drums with peripheral cooling fins 11 in. diameter, 3 in. wide.

BODYWORK

Five/six seater, four-door saloon body of pressed steel stressed skin construction, with aluminium doors, bonnet and boot lid.

ELECTRICAL SYSTEM

12-volt negative earth. Automatic regulation of dynamo current and voltage. Starter motor with planetary reduction gear. 55-ampere hour battery. Twin electric fuel pumps at rear of chassis. Double dipping head-lamps operated by foot switch. Twin fog lamps which also incorporate flashing filaments for direction indicators. Combined stop and tail lamps, with amber stop light lenses also functioning as flashing direction indicators.

DIMENSIONS

Wheelbase 10 ft. 3 in., Track front 4 ft. 10 in., rear 5 ft. 0in., Length 17 ft. 7¾ in., Width 6ft. 2¼ in., Height (unladen) 5 ft. 4 in., Turning circle 41 ft. 8 in.,

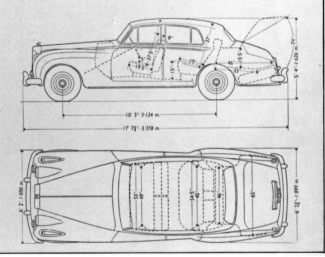

179. *Silver Cloud I* Standard Saloon. The most radically new Rolls-Royce model for 49 years, and the first with twin carburettors.
180. Long wheelbase Rolls-Royce *Silver Cloud* with division between the front and rear compartments.

181. Line-up of *Silver Clouds* at R.R.C.C. meeting in USA 1964.
182. 1958 Six-light Saloon by Hooper on the *Silver Coud I* long wheelbase chassis.

183. 1956 *Silver Cloud* Saloon by James Young.
184. Rolls-Royce *Silver Cloud I* Drophead Coupé by James Young.

185. Rolls-Royce *Silver Cloud I* Coupé-de-Ville by James Young.

186. Harold Radford estate car. These were built on the *Silver Cloud* chassis by H.J. Mulliner to Harold Radford's design after his own company ceased coachbuilding.

187. *Above* is H.J. Mulliner's superb Drophead Coupé, on the *Bentley* chassis (also produced with two or four doors on the *Silver Cloud* chassis). *Below* (188) *Silver Cloud* Drophead Coupé by James Young.

189. Another superb view of the *Silver Cloud* Standard Saloon showing the faultless style to advantage.
190. Apart from the radiator shell and bonnet lid the *'S'*-series *Bentley* coachwork is identical to that of the *Silver Cloud*.

191. *Bentley 'S' series Sports Saloon by H.J. Mulliner.*
192. *Bentley 'S' six-light Saloon.*

193. Beautiful facia panel of 'SI' Bentley. Note switch on steering column for Normal and Hard ride control.
194. A beautifully styled design by H.J. Mulliner on the 'S' series Continental chassis developed from their earlier 'R'-type design.

195. The Continental *'S'* series Sports Saloons: The four and two door designs by H.J. Mulliner. The four door design *below* (196) became known as the 'Flying Spur'. Note the unusual features of the car above, probably a one-off design.

197. Continental *'S' series* two door Sports Saloon. Above by James Young, *below* (198) by Park Ward.

199. James Young 'S' series *Bentley*: *above* Saloon with division on the long wheelbase chassis. *Below* (200), Sports Saloon on the Continental chassis.

201. Special features of the *Silver Cloud* 'Countryman' Saloon by Harold Radford (Coachbuilders) Ltd. Owned by Mr & Mrs E. Cheshire of Keilor, Victoria, Australia. A swivelling spot-lamp controlled from the driver's seat, is mounted on the front of the car to assist in reading sign-posts.

202. Compartments in the front doors accommodate water containers.

203. The rear seat folds flat to give extra luggage space, estate car style, when required.

118

204. *Top* The front seats slide forward and recline to make a particularly comfortable double bed.

205. *Centre* The 'Webasto' folding sunroof and tinted perspex draught-deflector.

206. *Left* The small picnic table folds out of a compartment in the boot while the two stools fit into the bumper over-riders.

207. *Above* All the comforts of home in a Countryman' Saloon. The compartments below the picnic trays contain decanters and glasses. The pipe rack can just be seen to the left of the off-side picnic tray.

208. Air-conditioning equipment.
209. Rolls-Royce refrigeration unit. The evaporator with a blower either side is installed right at the back of the boot. The whole installation is neatly covered in and not normally visible.

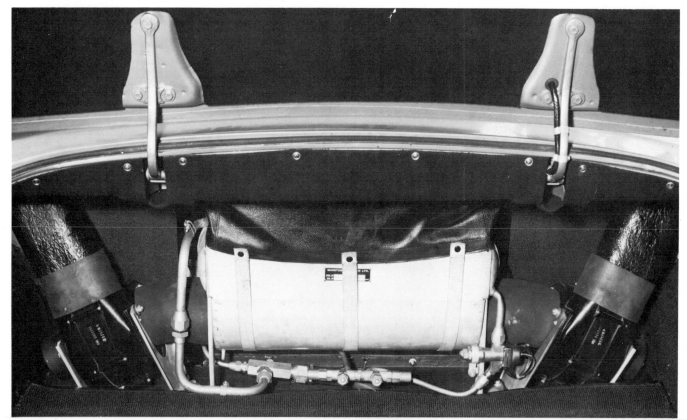

THE LONG WHEELBASE AND CONTINENTAL CHASSIS

For clients requiring a fast sports saloon or drophead coupé specialised coachwork was available on the 'S' series Bentley *Continental* chassis, which differed from the standard chassis in its higher rear axle ratio and the availability, until 1958, of a synchromesh gearbox. Limousine coachwork was available on the long wheelbase Rolls-Royce *Silver Cloud* or Bentley 'S' series chassis as an alternative to the long-established *Silver Wraith* limousines. A variety of specialised coachwork was also offered on the standard chassis.

THE V.8 ENGINE

The six cylinder 4,887 c.c. engine was used in the *Silver Cloud* for four years, and it was becoming more and more obvious that a need existed for more power to enable faster, smoother and quieter acceleration and cruising speeds, thus allowing the Rolls-Royce to compete with its American contemporaries. In actual fact the acceleration and silence of the 'six' left little to be desired, but the standard of silence which the Company set with its earlier models, (the most notable of these being the 40/50 h.p. *Silver Ghost*), was subject to strong trans-Atlantic competition. Generally speaking, a V.8 motor is smoother and quieter than a six, and, in 1959, Rolls-Royce announced that the *Silver Cloud I* was to be superseded by the *Silver Cloud II*, with a V.8 engine which the Company had been working on since 1947.

The new engine was formed by inserting cast-iron 'wet liners' into an aluminium block. No doubt Rolls-Royce would have liked to use a cast-iron block for the sake of silence, but a process for making them light enough was known only to the Americans (some Detroit cast-iron V.8's of similar capacity to the Rolls-Royce aluminium engine are actually lighter). The eight cylinders were arranged in a 90° vee with overhead pushrods and rockers and self-adjusting hydraulic tappets. A cubic capacity increase to 6,230 c.c. (380 cubic inches) resulted in a 30 per cent power increase, enabling the car to glide unobtrusively away with a light touch of the accelerator, or reach 30 m.p.h. in less than 3½ seconds, which is extremely fast, even by modern sports car standards. A top speed of over 110 m.p.h. could be effortlessly achieved. The ride in these cars is one of almost monotonous silence, and only a faint hum is evident when travelling at well over 100 m.p.h.

The new model resulted in various discreet improvements being made to the Rolls-Royce automatic transmission, which was a subject of constant experimentation and development at Crewe. The Company is not under the impression that their gearbox is perfect and will undoubtedly continue to experiment until it is quite right. Sir Henry Royce would not have been content with anything short of perfection had he lived to see the advent of the two-pedal automatic system in his beloved Rolls-Royce cars.

BODYWORK

The coachwork of the new *Silver Cloud* remained basically unchanged from that of the six-cylinder cars. Sitting inside the new cars one noticed that the speedometer was calibrated to 120 m.p.h. and that the steering wheel was smaller and more comfortably thin-

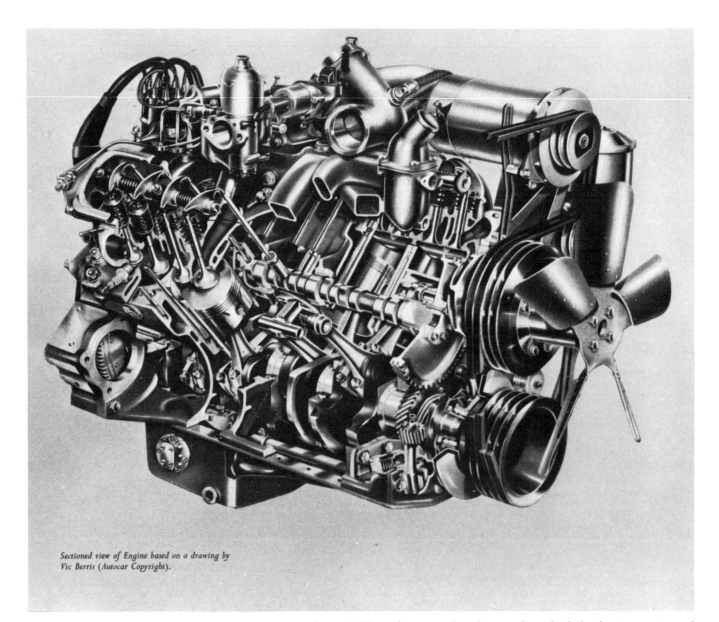

Sectioned view of Engine based on a drawing by Vic Berris (Autocar Copyright).

210. The Rolls-Royce light alloy V-8 engine as fitted to the *Silver Cloud II* and *III*, *Bentley S2* and *S3* and *Phantom V* models.

rimmed. New air vents placed at each end of the instrument panel capping rail enabled the occupants to direct air in any desired direction simply by moving neat louvres. Full refrigeration, electrically operated windows and 'Sundym' glass were available as extras, and, as with the *Silver Cloud I*, H.M.V. five-button radio, heating, demisting fresh-air system and electric fuel-filler cap were included as standard equipment. The *Silver Cloud II* and Bentley *S2* also had power-assisted steering included as a standard fitting.

SPECIAL COACHWORK

The long wheelbase and *Continental* chassis were retained, but with the new features, and were available with coachbuilt bodies similar to those previously available. Park Ward introduced a sleek new drophead coupé for the Bentley *Continental* chassis that was quite unlike anything previously offered, with the headlamps built into the ends of the straight-through wings.

211. *Bentley S2* chassis.
212. Rolls-Royce *Silver Cloud II* Saloon.

213. The *Bentley S2* Saloon. Externally the coachwork of the *Silver Cloud II* (previous page) and *Bentley S2* remained unchanged from that of the six-cylinder models.

214. *Bentley S2* Drophead Coupé with body work by Bentley Motors in conjunction with H.J. Mulliner and Co. Ltd.

215. *Bentley S2* Continental with coachwork by James Young.
216. A strikingly handsome design by H.J. Mulliner on the *S2* Continental chassis. Note the lowered radiator shell.

217. *Bentley S2* long wheelbase Saloon with division.

218. *Bentley S2* Continental Park Ward Drophead Coupé.

219. Controls of *S2* Continental Park Ward Drophead Coupé.

220. An early V-8 engine complete with automatic transmission and air-conditioning compressor.
221. A later (*S3*) V-8 showing the larger càrburettors.

The Phantom V

The long wheelbase 4.9 litre *Silver Wraith* was dropped from the range in 1958, to be replaced in 1959 with the latest in the line of *Phantoms*. The new 'large' Rolls, powered by the 6,230 c.c. aluminium V.8, released at the same time in the *Silver Cloud II*, was called the *Phantom V*, successor in name only to the exclusive *Phantom IV*. The *Phantom V* was considerably larger than the *Silver Wraith*, having a wheelbase of a full twelve feet and length only two inches short of twenty feet. Its weight (a full two and half tons!) and bulk are deceptive: the car is feather-light to steer and its performance only just falls short of that of the equivalent *Silver Clouds*, being capable of over 100 m.p.h. in virtual total silence. An impressive sight indeed was a *Phantom V* speeding down the M1 towards London before the days of the 70 m.p.h. limit!

In 1962 the *Phantom V* was modified in a similar fashion to the *Silver Cloud*. This involved a lower radiator and bonnet line, a four headlamp system and indicator lights recessed into the nose of the front wings. Raised compression and improved carburettors, like the *Silver Cloud,* improved the car's performance and economy.

The large chassis of the *Phantom V* enabled the coachbuilders to make the most of their traditional skills and build bodies to a standard of luxury and quality unparalleled by any other car produced in the world. The amount of legroom in the back of the *Phantom V* is phenomenal, even with the twin occasional seats in use. The Park Ward *Phantom V* could be furnished inside to suit individual requirements. Seats could be upholstered in West of England cloth or leather and the driver's seat is adjustable fore and aft. There is a heating and fresh air ventilation system with electrically operated windows and full refrigeration, available as an extra. The rear compartment is furnished with twin folding occasional seats and a cocktail cabinet is fitted behind the division. There is a radio in the rear compartment as well as in the front.

The James Young *Phantom V* was available in three forms, a seven-passenger limousine, a touring limousine and a Sedanca-de-Ville. These are, beyond doubt, the finest cars in the world, and are the pride of the last remaining independent coachbuilders for Rolls-Royce and Bentley cars. The James Young Centenary leaflet describes their *Phantom V* touring limousine thus: *This luxuriously equipped limousine is designed to provide the maximum comfort, whether owner or chauffeur driven. All door windows, the division and radio aerial are electrically operated. There are two occasional seats to the rear compartment. Both front and rear compartments are luxuriously upholstered in James Young special style with deep cushioning. Front compartment in leather, and rear in West of*

England cloth to client's choice. Deep pile carpet, and nylon rug to rear floor.

*The coachwork on this magnificent car is recognised as the finest to be found anywhere in the modern world. It is the culmination of a century of superb craftmanship which began with the Bromley Brougham.**

James Young *Phantom V* took Gold and Bronze medals at the 1965 Earls Court Motor Show, for their touring limousine and Sedanca-de-Ville respectively. H.J. Mulliner-Park Ward were awarded a Silver medal for their *Phantom V* seven-passenger limousine. This coachwork competition was held by the Institute of British Carriage and Automobile Manufacturers.

1966 prices for these cars were, including purchase tax, as follows:

Park Ward 7-passenger limousine	£9,517
James Young passenger limousine	£9,753
James Young Touring Limousine	£9,753

(James Young Sedanca-de-Ville and Park Ward State Landaulette prices on application.)

*The Bromley Brougham was a specialist product of James Young Ltd, during the last century.

222. Rolls-Royce *Phantom V* seven passenger Limousine by James Young.

PHANTOM V
CHASSIS NUMBERS

5AS 1–101	5VB 1–51
5AT 2–100	5VC 1–51
5BV 1–101	5VD 1–101
5CG 1–79	5VE 1–51
5VA 1–123	5VF 1–183

Up to and including the CG series, series starting with 1 use only odd numbers, while those starting with 2 use only evens. Number 13 not used. 'L' before chassis letter indicates left-hand drive car.

223. *Phantom V* chassis.
224. The Park Ward *Phantom V* seven passenger Limousine.

225. Interior of the Rolls-Royce *Phantom V* seven passenger by Park Ward.
226. *Phantom V* passenger's-eye view showing cocktail cabinet and occasional seats of this Park Ward seven passenger Limousine.

227. Original *Phantom V* styling by James Young. This special Sedanca-de-Ville was awarded 1st prize at Blenheim Palace in June 1962. A James Young car also received second prize.

228. 1963 *Phantom V* Touring Limousine by James Young.

229. Typical James Young luxury in a *Phantom V*.

230. James Young's *Phantom V* facia panel.

231. Hooper's swan-song. Design for the *Phantom V* chassis of which only one was built by Hoopers.

232. Three-quarter view of the *Phantom V* designed by Osmund F. Rivers of Hoopers for Mr Martin Martyn in the U.S. Built by Henri Chapron of Paris after Hoopers ceased coachbuilding.

233. *Phantom V* by Chapron, Paris.

THE PHANTOM V STATE LANDAULETTE

In the past, such eminent *Phantom V* clients as H.M. Queen Elizabeth the Queen Mother and His Excellency the Governor of Hong Kong have specified an opening Landaulette rear quarter on their Park Ward cars. At the 1966 Earl's Court Motor Show, H.J. Mulliner-Park Ward exhibited a new State Landaulette and announced that it would be available to governments requiring such a car. The entire rear compartment opened enabling passengers to stand in full view in processions, or sit on the back seat, which can be raised several inches. The features incorporated in these fine carriages can be seen in the illustrations.

234. The Rolls-Royce *Phantom V* State Landaulette. This magnificent H.J. Mulliner-Park Ward carriage is available to Heads of State and V.I.P.'s requiring a stately Landaulette for processional and ceremonial use. Clearly visible in this view are the flagmasts, fabric-covered roof over the front compartment and indicators on the sides of front wings.

235. Rear compartment of the State Landaulette. The rear seat can be raised 3 inches for ceremonial occasions.
236. Cocktail cabinet and occasional seats, *Phantom V* State Landaulette.

Engine	Eight cylinder 90° vee unit with overhead valves, hydraulic tappets, wet cylinder liners and cast aluminium cylinder block and heads.		**Chassis Lubrication**	Long life grease lubrication by nipples at 21 points.
Bore and Stroke	4·1 in. × 3·6 in. (104·14 mm. × 91·44 mm.).		**Electrical System**	*Ignition and distribution.* Automatic advance twin contact breakers. Firing order: A1, B1, A4, B4, B2, A3, B3, A2 ('A' is offside bank).
Cubic Capacity	380 cu. in.; 6230 c.c.			*Dynamo.* Maximum output 35 amperes at 13·5 volts.
Compression Ratio	9·0 : 1. (8·0 : 1 compression ratio engines can be supplied for countries where 100 octane fuel is not available.)			*Battery.* 12 volts, 67 amperes per hour at 20 hours rate.
Carburetters	Twin S.U., diaphragm type. Automatic choke for cold starting.		**Ventilation and Heating**	*Ventilation.* Fresh-air system. Air is ducted from an intake in the R.H. front wing to the windscreen and to adjustable outlets in the windscreen finishing rail. Amount and temperature are controllable through knobs on the fascia panel.
Fuel System	Twin S.U. electric independent pumps. Fuel tank capacity: 23 gallons (Imperial); 27·6 gallons (U.S.); 104·5 litres.			
Transmission	Rolls-Royce automatic gearbox with four forward speeds and reverse through epicyclic gears. Semi-floating rear axle with hypoid spiral final drive.			*Heating.* Recirculatory System. Air is recirculated from the rear compartment through a unit under the R.H. front wing to ducting over the front toeboard. A separate unit mixes fresh and saloon air and delivers it through a heater under the rear seat to outlets in the rear heelboard.
Overall Gear Ratios	1st speed 14·86 : 1 2nd speed 10·23 : 1 3rd speed 5·64 : 1 4th speed 3·89 : 1 Reverse 16·72 : 1			
Speed in Top Gear	22·5 m.p.h. per 1000 engine r.p.m.			*Defrosting.* Incorporated in ventilation system. Rear window electrically heated.
Brakes	Hydraulic and mechanical, servo assisted. As a safety measure, there are two entirely separate hydraulic systems and two master cylinders.			*Air Conditioning* (an optional extra). If desired the ventilation and heating systems may be augmented by a vapour compression cycle refrigeration system. The evaporator, under the rear parcel shelf, delivers cooled air into the rear compartment.
Tyre Sizes	8·90 × 15 in.			
Steering	Cam and roller, power assisted. 4¼ turns of the steering wheel from lock to lock.			
Suspension	*Front.* Independent front wheel suspension by coil springs controlled by hydraulic shock dampers. Anti-roll torsion bar. *Rear.* Asymmetric semi-elliptic leaf springs with hydraulic shock dampers electrically controlled through a switch on the steering column.		**Dimensions:**	*Wheelbase* 144 in. *Turning Circle* 48 ft. 9 in. *Track, front* 5 ft. 0⅞ in. *Track, rear* 5 ft. 4 in. For body dimensions, please see separate plans.

The Silver Cloud III
and Bentley S3

In 1962 the final change in the *Silver Cloud* and Bentley *S* models took place, the result being the *Silver Cloud III* and Bentley *S3*. The main change was in the reshaping of the front, best described by the Rolls-Royce and Bentley brochure on these cars: *The new four head-lamp system incorporated in the redesigned frontal appearance provides more illumination at a greater distance ahead and at the same time more effectively lights the sides of the road. Flashing indicators and side lamps are combined in a single unit mounted in the nose of the front wings. The height of the radiator is reduced and the bonnet top has increased slope which improves the forward vision for the driver.* Other changes to the coachwork included a wider back seat with increased legroom, new individual front seat cushions, and a padded capping rail over the fascia. The bumper over-riders were reshaped, apparently to blend better with the lowered front end, although the coachbuilt models retained the older pattern. Full re-frigeration, electric window lifts, electric wing aerial and 'Sundym' glass were available if required.

The Editor of the monthly *Motor Sport* had the following to say of the *Silver Cloud III*: . . . . *but it cannot be too strongly emphasised that at three-figure speeds, to a maximum of 114 m.p.h., the quiet-ness level remains virtually the same as it is at 30 m.p.h., so that the volume of the radio does not need to be increased. This is an ex-tremely impressive factor which justifies the considerable cost of the Rolls-Royce.* He went on to say that at £5,632, the price of a new *Cloud* is quite incidental, even moderate.

Rolls-Royce enthusiasts have every reason to mourn the passing of the *Silver Cloud* in favour of the more modern concepts of the *Silver Shadow*; the irresistable appeal of these superb motor cars will linger for many years to come. Although the more practical *Silver Shadow* is the *Cloud's* logical and inevitable successor, it is perhaps unfortuate that the old model was not continued in produc-tion alongside the new, thus offering the client a choice without his having to resort to costly individual specialist coachwork.

SPECIALISED COACHWORK

The H.J.Mulliner Long Wheelbase Saloon with division was altered to conform with the standard saloon. This and other specialised coachwork is admirably described in the Rolls-Royce and Bentley catalogue:

A two-door, a four-door and a drophead coupé with hand-built coachwork by H.J. Mulliner-Park Ward Ltd, on the Silver Cloud III *chassis are available for the owner who requires a car of particular distinction. The coachwork is constructed of steel and light alloy by*

237. The Rolls-Royce *Silver Cloud III* chassis as exhibited at Earls Court.

skilled craftsmen and represents all the traditional skills of the coach-builder.

The four-door saloon has graceful and distinctive lines and is designed to seat four persons in great comfort. There are two individual bucket seats in the front with a folding centre armrest between them. A special curved walnut veneered fascia panel prevents reflections on the wide wrap-round wind-screen. The door garnish rails are also walnut veneer. The large boot has the spare wheel, tool kit and battery under the floor.

The long wheelbase saloon with division is designed for the owner who requires a limousine car for business use, yet can be used as a saloon at other times. It is available on either the Silver Cloud III or Bentley S3 chassis which has been lengthened by four inches. Chauffeur-driven with the electrically operated division raised, the owner may carry on a confidential conversation or prepare notes in complete privacy. Apart from the longer wheelbase the engine details are similar to the saloon.

The increase of four inches aft of the centre pillar gives improved access through the larger rear doors and more legroom in the rear compartment. The centre panel contains controls for the heater, a switch to raise and lower the division glass, a cigar lighter and a volume control for the rear radio loudspeaker.

238. The re-styled standard coachwork for the *Silver Cloud III*. Note the increased slope of the bonnet down to the lowered radiator shell, twin headlamps, re-styled front wings and smaller bumper over-riders.

239. The instrument panel of the *Silver Cloud III*.

240. The *Bentley S3* Saloon.
241. *Silver Cloud III*. Reprinted from catalogue.

242. *Silver Cloud III* Saloon by H.J. Mulliner. Based on the 'Flying Spur' coachwork originally designed for the *Bentley* Continental.
Silver Shadow.

243. Instrument panel of *Silver Cloud III* Sports Saloon by H.J. Mulliner.

The H.J. Mulliner-Park Ward four-door saloon, two-door saloon and drophead coupé were also available on the Bentley *S3 Continental* chassis and were derived from earlier H.J. Mulliner and Park Ward designs. The four-door Bentley *Continental* by H.J. Mulliner-Park Ward was known as the 'Flying Spur' and was derived from the original H.J. Mulliner design first introduced on the *S1 Continental* chassis. The Mulliner two-door saloon and drophead coupé were produced in *S3* form for a while then dropped in favour of Park Ward styles.

James Young Ltd, of Bromley retained their Bentley *Continental* styles and made the same coachwork styles available on the *Silver Cloud III* chassis to the client's choice. Their limousine coachwork for the *Silver Cloud III* long wheelbase chassis was re-styled to resemble their *Phantom V* designs.

244. *Silver Cloud III* two door Saloon by Park Ward.
245. *Silver Cloud III* Drophead Coupé by Park Ward.

246. H.J. Mulliner continued to adapt the standard coachwork into an attractive Drophead Coupé.
247. *Below*, the two door version.

248. *Bentley S3* Continental. This superb car with coachwork by H.J. Mulliner is known as the 'Flying Spur'.

249. A variation of H.J. Mulliner's *S3* 'Flying Spur' Sports Saloon. Note smaller rear quarter lights.

250. *Bentley S3* Continental two door Saloon by Park Ward.
251. *Bentley S3* Continental Drophead Coupé, hood erected.

252. 1963 *Bentley S3* Continental Saloon by James Young.
253. *Silver Cloud III* two door Sports Saloon by James Young. This car also has a Continental specification.

254. *Silver Cloud III* with two door Saloon built for King Faisal of Iraq on long wheelbase chassis by James Young.
255. 1963 *Silver Cloud III* long wheelbase Saloon with division by James Young.

ROLLS-ROYCE SILVER CLOUD II & III AND BENTLEY S2 & S3 IN PRODUCTION 1959-1966

ENGINE

Eight cylinders in two rows forming 90° vee. Bore 4.1 inches, stroke 3.6 inches, 6,230 c.c., firing order A1, B1, A4, B4, B2, A3, B3, A2. (A = off-side bank) overhead valves, hydraulic tappets, aluminium alloy block and cylinder heads, twin S.U. carburettors, twin S.U. fuel pumps.

TRANSMISSION

Rolls-Royce automatic gearbox:

Ratios: *1st,* 3.82:1, *2nd,* 2.63:1, *3rd,* 1.45:1, *Top,* 1:1.

Divided propeller shaft with universal joints connecting the two halves. Hypoid bevel final drive with four star differential and semi-floating half shafts.

Ratio: 3.08:1. (2.92:1 on *S2 Continentals*)

SUSPENSION

Front: Coil spring independent with hydraulic shock dampers.

Rear: Semi-elliptic with hydraulic shock dampers controlled by switch on steering wheel.

BRAKES

Internal expanding drum, servo assisted, hydraulic front, mechanical rear, with a second hydraulic circuit on both front and rear.

CHASSIS LUBRICATION

Long life grease lubrication by nipples at 21 points.

STEERING

Cam and roller, power assisted.

WHEELS

15″ carrying 8.20 x 15 tyres.

PRINCIPAL DIMENSIONS

Wheelbase: 10′ 3″ (Long wheelbase 10′ 7″)

Front Track: 4′ 10″

Rear Track: 5′ 0″

Turning Circle: 42′ 0″

The number of cars produced has not been revealed.

Silver Cloud III Performance Figures:

Australian 'Motor Manual' July 1965

Acceleration:

From rest to 30 mph through gears			3.3 secs
,,	,, ,, 40 mph	,, ,,	5.3 secs
,,	,, ,, 50 mph	,, ,,	7.7 secs
,,	,, ,, 60 mph	,, ,,	10.5 secs
,,	,, ,, 70 mph	,, ,,	13.7 secs
,,	,, ,, 80 mph	,, ,,	18.8 secs
,,	,, ,, 90 mph	,, ,,	25.5 secs
,,	,, ,,100 mph	,, ,,	34.5 secs

Speeds in gears:

Top: 116.3 mph

3rd: 70 mph

2nd: 40 mph

1st: 25 mph

Fuel consumption: 12.2 m.p.g.

CHASSIS NUMBERS

Silver Cloud II, 1959–1962
SPA2–326, SRA1–325
STB2–500, SVB1–501
SWC2–730, SXC1–671
SYD2–550, SZD1–551
SAE1–685
Long Wheelbase Silver Cloud II
1959–1962
LCA1–76
LCB1–101
LCC1–101
LCD1–25
Bentley *S2*, 1959–1962
B1AA–B325AA

B2AM–B326AM
B1BR–B501BR
B2BS–B500BS
B1CT–B445CT
B2CU–B756CU
B1DV–B501DV
B2DW–B376DW
Long Wheelbase S2, 1959–1962
LBA1–26
LBB1–33
Continental S2, 1959–1962
BC1AR–BC151AR
BC1BY–BC101BY
BC1CZ–BC139CZ

Silver Cloud III, 1962–1966
SAZ1–61
SCX1–877
SDW1–601
SEV1–495
SFU1–803
SGT1–659
SHS1–357
SJR1–623
SKP1–423
CSC1–93B
CSC1–81C

Long Wheelbase Silver Cloud III
1962–1965
CAL1–83
CLB1–61
CCL1–101
CDL1–95
CEL1–105
CFL1–41
CGL1–29

Bentley *S3*, 1962–1965
B2AV–B26AV
B2CN–B828CN
B2DF–B198DF
B2EC–B530EC
B2FG–B350FG
B2GJ–B200GJ
B2HN–B400HN
B2JP–B40JP

Long Wheelbase S3, 1962–1965
BAL2–30
BBL2–12
BCL2–22
Continental S3, 1962–1966
BC2XA–BC174AXA
BC2XB–BC100XB
BC2XC–BC202XC
BC2XD–BC28XD
BC2XE–BC120XE

With the exception of the *S2* long wheelbase and *Continental* series, series starting with 1 use only odd numbers, while series starting with 2 use only evens. Number 13 not used. 'L' before chassis letters indicates a left-hand drive car.

The Most Radically New Rolls-Royce Cars for 59 Years

The Rolls-Royce and Bentley have been fundamentally redesigned. All that they now have in common with the cars they replace is the recently introduced (and now modified) 6,230 c.c. eight cylinder power unit. Why this radical change? Because nothing less could fully translate Rolls-Royce motoring into the terms of heavy traffic and modern roads.

The Silver Shadow *and Bentley* T *series will cruise at high speeds in silence and with complete safety and controlability. They can be driven very fast even over rough, steeply-cambered European roads. And yet they have every quality that fits a car for the life of a modern city: effortless handling and flexibility in traffic, great comfort, swift and simple parking.*

This kind of all-round performance requires the full use of the most modern automobile technology. But for Rolls-Royce performance can never be enough. It is the manner of the performance that counts. That is why ten years of intensive development have gone into making all independent suspension, automatic height control, power disc brakes, power steering and automatic transmission work to Rolls-Royce standards.

In short: these cars combine advanced engineering and safety specifications with traditional Rolls-Royce standards of craftsmanship. In the manner of their performance they are as revolutionary as the Silver Ghost *was 59 years ago.*

The above is taken from a Rolls-Royce and Bentley advertisement which appeared in the *Autocar* of October 8th, 1965. This advertisement was very comprehensive and familiarised the public with the new features included in the specifications of the car. The main modifications were as follows:

New Proportions:

The *Silver Shadow* and Bentley *T* series are lower and more compact than their predecessors. The *Silver Shadow* is 6¾ inches shorter, 4½ inches lower and 3¾ inches narrower than the *Silver Cloud*.

Most of this shortening is in the bonnet, the one piece lid of which is hinged along its leading edge, in contrast to the previous Rolls-Royce practice of hinging two separate side panels along the central strip. The passenger cabin is similar in length to that of the *Silver Cloud* and improvements in legroom seem to have been achieved by a reduction in seat cushion widths. Although the armrest-to-armrest dimension of the front compartment remains unaltered the seats are much narrower and the resultant central gap is occupied by folding

256. *Silver Shadow.*

armrests and electric seat adjustment controls. There seems little point in this and the author prefers the *Silver Cloud III* front seats, which are extremely comfortable and support the occupant well. The reduction to conventional modern car proportions has been made at the expense of the superb high driving position so characteristic of previous models. A transmission hump renders the car a four-seater; however, this is most pronounced in the front compartment where a third occupant is not a feasible proposition. The rear seat is shaped to seat two in luxury and is furnished with a folding central armrest with a small oddments compartment under a hinged lid.

The interior is luxuriously equipped with the usual Rolls-Royce features, including folding picnic tables and illuminated vanity mirrors. All traditional materials are used with the exception of the headlining which is now trimmed with a 'durable washable material'.

The general effect of the overall reduction and restyling is in the impression it creates visually. The Rolls-Royce no longer stands out from other cars and has lost a great deal of its grandeur and splendour. However, the best interests of the clients were at heart and an excellent compromise has been achieved.

Monocoque construction:

The *Silver Shadow* is the first Rolls-Royce with no chassis. The conventional chassis frame is replaced by a front sub-assembly which carries the engine and other front-end mechanics, a rear sub-assembly for the back axle and suspension, with the final drive unit carried on a flexibly-mounted cross-member.

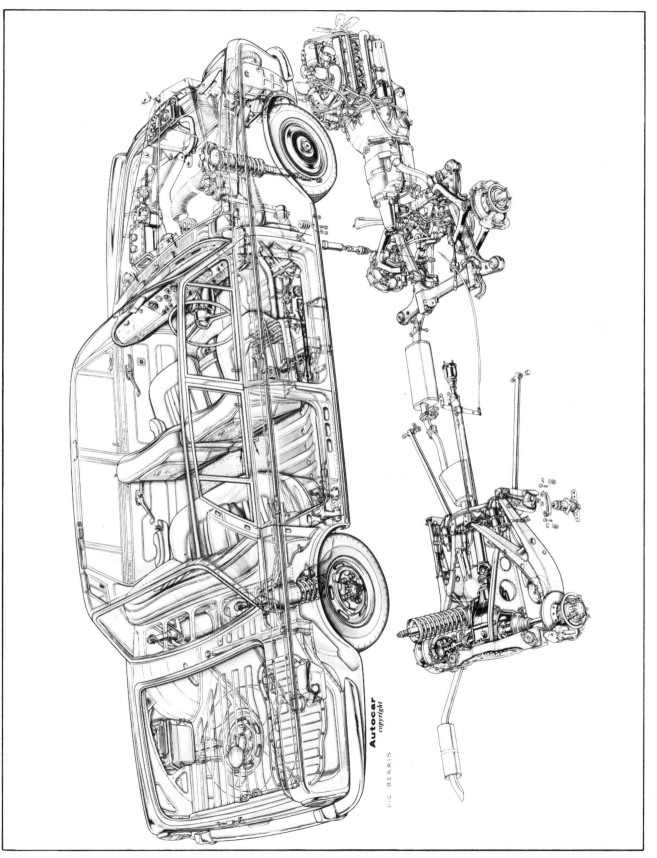

Autocar
copyright

VIC BERRIS

257. The Rolls-Royce *Silver Shadow* chassis.

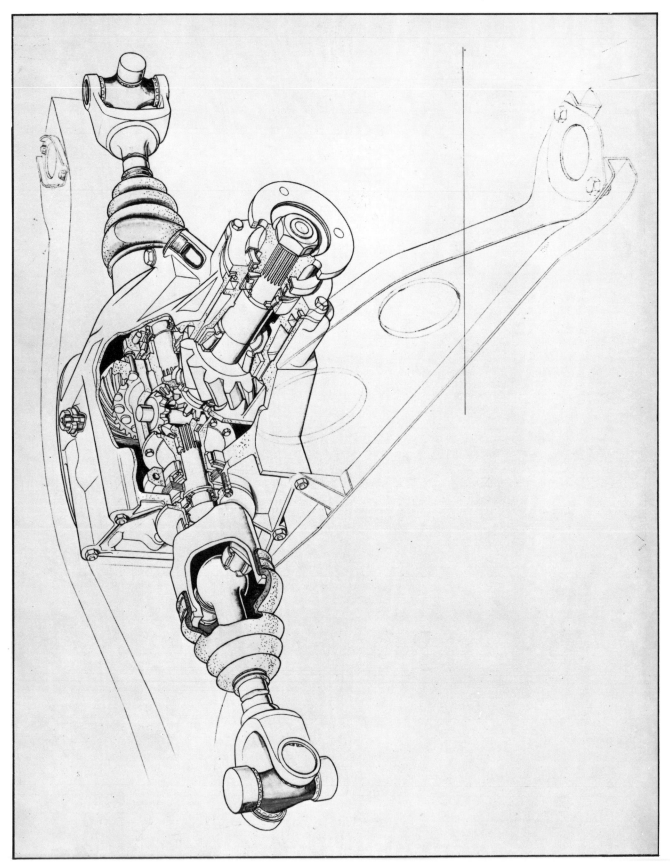

258. The rear axle arrangement of *Silver Shadow* and *Bentley 'T'* series.

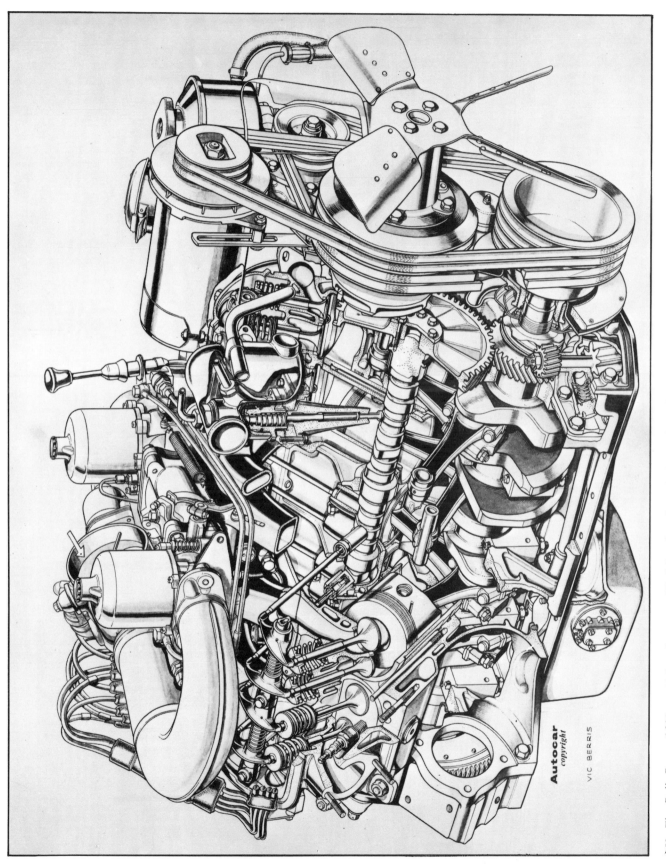

259. The Rolls-Royce 6,230 c.c. V-8 engine as modified for the *Silver Shadow* and *Bentley 'T'* series.

Autocar
copyright

VIC BERRIS

Four Wheel Independent Suspension:

By 1936 the Rolls-Royce *Phantom* was enhanced by the admirable innovation of independent front suspension, and it took nearly thirty years to make independent rear wheel suspension work to exacting Rolls-Royce standards. Suspension and hydraulic self-levelling components are mounted on the front and rear subframes.

Hydraulic Self-levelling:

The all-independent suspension is complimented by an intricate hydraulic self-levelling system which maintains a constant level to the car regardless of the weight and distribution of the load. This system operates at two distinct speeds: slowly when travelling, so as not to affect the normal functioning of the independent suspension, and almost simultaneously when standing still with a door open or neutral gear selected. The system is operated by a pump driven from the engine, with hydraulic fluid from a reservoir which also serves the brake circuits. In consequence the traditional Rolls-Royce 'ride control' has been eliminated.

Hydraulic Disc Brakes:

In association with Girling, Rolls-Royce developed disc brakes which are as quiet, progressive and fade-free as their old mechanical servo-drums. As on the *Silver Cloud*, the new cars have three independent brake circuits, two powered from the self-levelling system providing 77 per cent of the total braking, and a direct mastercylinder circuit to give the driver 'feel' in the brake pedal. Another well-known and long established feature of the Rolls-Royce is the gearbox-driven friction-disc brake servo, and this has also been eliminated on the *Silver Shadow*.

A New System of Power Assisted Steering:

The effort required to drive the latest Rolls-Royce or Bentley is reduced even further by an improved power assistance system incorporating a rotary valve integral steering box and Saginaw (U.S.) lowfriction recirculating ball. The modernised two-spoke steering wheel retains its discreet black finish, central horn button and comfortable thin rim.

The 6,230 c.c. V8 Engine:

The output of the 6.23 litre eight-cylinder light alloy power unit has been raised but the actual figure is not yet available from the manufacturers. The cylinder head is redesigned with larger ports and the sparking plugs are now accessible from above, relieving the mechanic or chauffeur of the tiresome task of removing the front wheels to reach them.

Electric Gear Selection:

The Rolls-Royce four speed automatic transmission now has free wheel on second and first gears, inoperative when second is selected for engine braking. The range selector lever, which still projects from right of the steering column, is extremely light in its action because of an electric gear selecting mechanism; this should satisfy those who complained that the previous selector lever was stiff and clumsy. *R, N, 4, 3, 2,* are now visible in a window above the steering column. The *Silver Cloud* 'extras', electrically operated windows and wing aerial, are standard equipment on the *Silver Shadow* and the refrigerated air-conditioning unit is still an option.

The *Silver Shadow*, as in the case of its noble predecessors, makes no concessions to frivolous styling fads. Although it may be said that it lacks a 'certain something' that the *Silver Cloud* possessed, the *Shadow* has reverted to *Silver Dawn* compactness. At the same time, it provides considerably more room for passengers, luggage and such creature comforts as are required by the present generation of Rolls-Royce customers, a large percentage of whom are Americans.

260. Rolls-Royce *Silver Shadow* and *Bentley 'T'* series Standard Saloon.

261. *Silver Shadow* two door Sports Saloon by H.J. Mulliner-Park Ward.
262. *Silver Shadow* Drophead Coupé by H.J. Mulliner-Park Ward.

263. Rolls-Royce *Silver Shadow* Drophead Coupé by H.J. Mulliner-Park Ward. The dashboard can clearly be seen.

264. *Bentley 'T'* series two door Sports Saloon by Pininfarina. Exhibited at Earls Court Motor Show, 1968.

265. 1966 *Bentley 'T'* series two door Sports Saloon by James Young; the final design of that company.

266. Rolls-Royce *Silver Shadow* long wheelbase Saloon with division by H.J. Mulliner-Park Ward. Note leather cloth covered roof.

160

Recent Developments at Crewe

The first modifications to the *Silver Shadow* and *'T'* series cars were made in 1968 to conform to U.S. safety requirements. The modifications affected the front seats which are now wider and heavily padded on the backs of the squabs, (the traditional picnic tables being removed in the interest of safety), the instrument panel is now surrounded by a better, more effective crash-pad, and traffic indicator and brake light repeaters are now fitted to the wings. A spring-loaded collapsible 'Spirit of Ecstasy' can be specified for countries where her former upright rigidity is now illegal.

By fitting the improved *Silver Shadow* engine and providing separate refrigeration units for front and rear compartments the *Phantom V* has become the *Phantom VI,* probably the last Rolls-Royce to be built on a conventional chassis frame.

Great steps have been taken by the Company regarding exhaust emission control. The present U.S. export cars comply with the latest American standards for the control of air pollution from motor vehicles. The extra equipment fitted comprises a mixture-weakening device and an air injection system. The mixture weakening device allows cleaner mixture at part-throttle while the air injection system introduces air into the exhaust ports to help complete the combustion of unburnt gases. The vacuum advance on the distributor is deleted together with other modifications to the ignition system.

The stroke of the latest *Silver Shadows* has been increased to 99.1 m.m. giving a capacity of 6,750 c.c., the extra power available being partly absorbed by the refrigeration compressor and emission control devices.

The Rolls-Royce four-speed fluid flywheel automatic transmission introduced in 1952 has been replaced in recent *Shadows* by a more efficient three-speed torque converter unit. Current Rolls-Royces and Bentleys now have a top speed in the region of 130 m.p.h. with acceleration to match.

As from March 1971 the Company has a new form. The Motor Car Division has become Rolls-Royce Motors Ltd (also incorporating the former Oil Engine Division). With this change, brought about as· a result of the Company passing into receivership, came the *Corniche,* the fastest Rolls-Royce ever. Outwardly this fine new model is basically the coachbuilt H.J. Mulliner-Park Ward two-door car (drophead coupé or saloon) with a slightly deeper radiator shell and interior decor incorporating a small-diameter wood-rimmed steering wheel requiring only three and a half turns to swing the big car from lock-to-lock.

The current models have erased any doubt that may have existed that the Rolls-Royce is still 'The Best Car in the World'. No car in the world combines luxury and sporting car characteristics in quite

The Rolls-Royce Phantom VI is a seven seat limousine with coachwork by H. J. Mulliner, Park Ward. Superlative comfort for the occupants has been the aim of the designers of this distinguished motor car, and so the beautifully appointed rear compartment provides particularly spacious and luxurious accommodation for three passengers. Two occasional seats fold out from the lower half of the division when required. An important standard feature is an advanced air conditioning system which incorporates two refrigeration units.

The excellent road performance of the Phantom VI is derived from a 6230 cc V-8 engine similar to that of the Silver Shadow. A fully-automatic transmission, power assisted steering, and a breaking system combining two hydraulic circuits and a mechanical linkage are all included in the standard specification.

The Phantom VI is also available with landaulette coachwork by H. J. Mulliner, Park Ward.

ROLLS-ROYCE LIMITED
MOTOR CAR DIVISION
CREWE CHESHIRE

Printed in England T.V.P   TSD 2514

the same manner as the new cars from Crewe, which have taken their name from the experimental streamlined sporting Bentley saloon destroyed on the docks at Dieppe during a war-time bomb attack.

268. Rolls-Royce *Corniche* two door Saloon by H.J. Mulliner-Park Ward.
269. Rolls-Royce *Corniche* Convertible.

Rolls-Royce Corniche

WHY CORNICHE?

Corniche is that part of the South Coast of France between Nice and
Italy which contains the Principality of Monaco and the town of Monte
Carlo, which has always been a popular resort with English people.
Ever since the early days of motoring the grand touring car has been
developed to enable travel across the Continent to be undertaken in
comfort, particularly before motorways were built. It was the Hon. C.S.
Rolls who saw the need for a car capable of making the journey and he
persuaded Sir Henry Royce to embark on the 40/50h.p. Silver Ghost
models in 1907 with this journey in mind.

A Corniche car was built before the outbreak of the last war. It
was a prototype Mark V Bentley and was fitted with a body by Van
Vooren of Paris. It had just completed it's 15,000 mile (24000km.)
endurance testing when war was declared and it was destroyed by a
bomb on the quayside (six years later the R.A.C. port representative
at Dieppe returned the keys to the company). Plans for production
of the Corniche were abandoned because of the war.

The name, 'Corniche' has been chosen for the latest Rolls-Royce
and Bentley coachbuilt models because it symbolises their high
cruising speeds and their ability to cover great distances with the
minimum of fatigue.

With the introduction of the new cars, the name 'Silver Shadow' will
refer only to the four door saloon and long wheelbase saloon. Thus,
the full range of Rolls-Royce and Bentley models is now:

Rolls-Royce Silver Shadow four-door saloon.

Rolls-Royce Silver Shadow long wheelbase saloon with or without
 a division.

Rolls-Royce Corniche two-door saloon.

Rolls-Royce Corniche convertible.

Rolls-Royce Phantom VI limousine.

Bentley T Series four-door saloon.

Bentley Corniche two-door saloon.

Bentley Corniche convertible.

ROLLS-ROYCE LIMITED
MOTOR CAR DIVISION

PRESS INFORMATION

Public Relations Department · Crewe, Cheshire · Telephone Crewe 55155 · Telex 36121

E. R. NICHOLSON, RECEIVER AND MANAGER,
APPOINTED 4th FEBRUARY, 1971.

ROLLS-ROYCE AND BENTLEY CORNICHE TWO-DOOR SALOON AND
CONVERTIBLE MODELS INTRODUCED

Rolls-Royce today introduce the Corniche two-door saloon and convertible - both motor cars with hand-built coachwork by Rolls-Royce's subsidiary company, H.J. Mulliner, Park Ward. Although developed from the Rolls Royce Silver Shadow and Bentley T Series two-door saloons and convertibles they supersede, the Corniche models offer a considerable improvement in performance as a result of increased engine power.

Modifications to the 6750 cc aluminium engine to give 10% more power are basically changes to the valve and ignition timing, a more efficient air silencer and a low loss exhaust system increased in diameter from 2.0 inches (5.1 cm) to 2.25 inches (5.7 cm). A minor change is an increase in the cooling fan drive ratio.

The Corniche engine gives the motor car much improved acceleration particularly at overtaking speeds of between 50 and 100 mph (80 and 161 km/h). It also gives the Corniche the ability to cruise at very high speeds and the car is particularly suitable for long distance touring. Maximum speed is in excess of 120 mph (193 km/h). The new engine is even quieter then the previous power unit.

The overall styling of the Corniche models is similar to their predecessors but many detail changes have been made in keeping with the car's more sporting character. The re-designed facia has a full set of instruments, including a tachometer, situated in front of the driver. A 15 inch (38 cm) diameter steering wheel has the effect of further improving the directional stability of the car at the higher cruising speeds of which it is capable.

External distinguishing features are a 0.47 inch (11.9 mm) deeper radiator shell, new wheel trims which are designed to give an optimum flow of cooling air to the disc brakes, rectangular reversing lamps which blend with the overall shape of the rear of the car, and a Corniche name plate on the boot lid.

The advanced chassis specification is similar to that of the Rolls-Royce Silver Shadow four-door and long wheelbase saloons and includes four wheel independent suspension, three separate braking systems, automatic ride height control, automatic transmission and power assisted steering.

The coachwork by H.J. Mulliner, Park Ward is built, trimmed and finished by craftsmen to the highest standards of traditional English coachbuilding. The Corniche is extremely well appointed and the customer can exercise a wide choice of finishes, trim materials and optional equipment to meet his own personal requirements. Full air conditioning is part of the standard specification.

Press Enquiries to D.E.A. Miller–Williams, Rolls–Royce Limited, 14–15 Conduit St. W.1. Telephone: 01.629.6201 (office) Bishops (0279).51389 (home)

270. The superb driving compartment of the *Corniche*. Note the optional 'speed control' system controls to the right of the steering wheel.

SILVER SHADOW AND BENTLEY 'T' SERIES IN PRODUCTION 1965 TO PRESENT

ENGINE

Eight cylinders arranged in 90° vee with 4.1 inch bore by 3.6 inch stroke giving 6,230 c.c. (380 cu. in.) *1968* U.S. market cars 3.9 inch stroke, 6,750 c.c. (412 cu. in.) *1969* larger capacity engine standard. Compression ratio 9: 1 (8: 1 available where 100 octane fuel unavailable.) Firing order A1, B1, A4, B4, B2, A3, B3, A2 ('A' being the right-hand bank when looking forward). Overhead valve gear pushrod operated through hydraulically self-adjusting tappets. Two S.U. carburettors.

TRANSMISSION

Four-speed epicyclic automatic gearbox with electrical over-riding hand control and range selection from steering column lever. Gear ratios *1st,* 3.82: 1, *2nd,* 2.63: 1, *3rd,* 1.45: 1, *4th,* 1.00: 1, *reverse,* 4.3: 1. *1968* (U.S. export cars) and *1969* (standard) torque converter three-speed automatic gearbox. Gear ratios *1st,* 2.48: 1, *2nd,* 1.48: 1, *3rd,* 1.00: 1, *reverse,* 2.08: 1. Propeller shaft with needle rolling bearing universal joints. Hypoid bevel final drive, ratio 3.08: 1.

PRINCIPAL DIMENSIONS
Overall length: 16′ 11½″
Overall height: 4′ 11¾″ (Standard saloon)
Overall width: 5′ 11″ (Standard saloon)
Wheelbase: 9′ 11½″
Front track 4′ 9½″
Rear track 4′ 9½″
Turning circle 38′ 0″

BRAKES

Discs to all four wheels. Triple hydraulic system incorporating two independent power circuits and one direct master cylinder circuit. One power system operates one caliper on each front disc and part of the rear brake, while the other operates the other caliper on each front disc. The direct master-cylinder circuit provides the rest of the rear braking. A deceleration conscious, pressure limiting valve prevents premature rear wheel locking. Mechanical handbrake with equalising link operating rear disc calipers.

HYDRAULIC SYSTEM

Two underbonnet accumulators, maintained at 2,500 p.s.i. to operate power brakes and automatic height control system, two underbonnet reservoirs and two camshaft driven piston pumps.

SUSPENSION

Four-wheel independent:

Front: double wishbones, coil springs and hydraulic telescopic dampers; incorporating anti-dive characteristics.

Rear: trailing arms, coil springs and hydraulic telescopic dampers; incorporating anti-lift characteristics.

Two-speed automatic height-control operated by engine driven hydraulic pump maintains optimum riding height and attitude regardless of loading. Fast height control when doors or neutral gear selected.

STEERING

Power assisted, rotary valve, integral ram steering box. Mechanical elements by low-friction recirculating ball. Four turns lock-to-lock

1970 Three and three-quarter turns lock-to-lock

1972 Three and a quarter turns lock-to-lock.

CHASSIS

Monocoque construction with front and rear sub-frames to carry engine, suspension etc. Sub-frames attached to body by resilient metal mountings.

1972 Rubber mountings. Greasing required at steering and height-control ball joints every 12,000 miles. All other joints sealed for life.

WHEELS

15 inch steel disc wheels on five studs carrying 8.15 x 15 low profile tyres. *1972* Radial ply tyres 205 x 15.

ELECTRICAL SYSTEM

Electrical operation of gear selection, front seat adjustment, windows, rear window demister, wing aerial, windscreen wipers and washers, cigar lighters front and rear, petrol filler flap, heater, demister and refrigeration controls (when fitted). Warning lights for hydraulic accumulator pressure, engine oil pressure, coolant level, fuel level, ignition, handbrake/stop light bulb failure, hazard warning system. Air-conditioning available as extra at first but later made standard.

U.K. PRICES

1968	Standard saloon	£ 7,960
	H. J. Mulliner, Park Ward two-door saloon	£10,644
	H. J. Mulliner, Park Ward drophead coupé	£11,166
	Bentley 'T' series standard saloon	£ 7,895
	Bentley 'T' series	
	H. J. Mulliner, Park Ward two-door saloon	£10,574
	Bentley 'T' series	
	H. J. Mulliner, Park Ward drophead coupé	£11,101
1973	Rolls-Royce or Bentley standard saloon	£10,406
	Long Wheelbase saloon	£11,944
	Long Wheelbase limousine	£12,737

271. The inner box structure of the monocoque body is manufactured from rust-protected high-grade mild steel. Additional strength is applied to drophead coupé bodies.

272. The main body panels contribute a strength factor, and are produced in 20 s.w.g. steel. Wings, as shown here, are welded, hammered and turned on jigs by experts.

273. These H.J. Mulliner-Park Ward craftsmen are engaged in the jigging and welding operations by which the body panels are applied to the steel box structure that forms the basis of a modern coach-built motorcar.

274. Since the rigidity in the box structure of the body is essential, the wings, scuttle and roof are fabricated in steel. Doors, bonnet and bootlid, which do not add to the rigidity of the car, are made of aluminium. At each stage during the manufacture of the body shell there is meticulous inspection of all jigging, welding and clearances.

CORNICHE
IN PRODUCTION 1971 TO PRESENT

ENGINE

Eight cylinders arranged in 90° vee with 4.1 inch bore by 3.9 inch stroke giving 6,750 c.c. (412 cu. in.) Compression ratio 9:1 Firing order A1, B1, A4, B4, B2, A3, B3, A2 ('A' being the right-hand bank when looking forward). Overhead valve gear push-rod operated through hydraulically self-adjusting tappets. Two S.U. HD.8 carburettors.

TRANSMISSION

Three-speed torque converter automatic gearbox with electrical over-riding hand control and range selection from steering column lever. Gear ratios *1st,* 2.48:1, *2nd,* 1.48:1, *3rd,* 1.00:1, *reverse,* 2.08:1. One-piece propeller shaft with one ball and trunnion constant velocity universal joint and one needle roller-bearing Hooks universal joint. Hypoid bevel final drive, ratio 3.08:1.

BRAKES

Eleven inch brakes to all four wheels. Triple hydraulic system incorporating two independent power circuits and one direct master-cylinder circuit. One power system operates one caliper on each front disc and part of the rear brake, while the other operates the other caliper on each front disc. The direct master-cylinder circuit provides the rest of the rear braking. A deceleration conscious, pressure limiting valve prevents premature rear wheel locking. Mechanical handbrake with equaliser link operating rear disc calipers.

HYDRAULIC SYSTEM

Two underbonnet accumulators, maintained at 2,500 p.s.i. to operate power brakes and automatic height control system, two underbonnet reservoirs and two camshaft driven piston pumps.

SUSPENSION

Four wheel independent:

Front: double wishbones, coil springs and hydraulic telescopic dampers; incorporating anti-dive characteristics.

Rear: trailing arms, coil springs and hydraulic telescopic dampers; incorporating anti-lift characteristics.

Two-speed automatic height-control operated by engine driven hydraulic pump maintains optimum riding height and attitude regardless of loading. Fast height control when doors open or neutral gear selected.

STEERING

Power assisted, rotary valve, integral ram steering box. Mechanical elements by low-friction recirculating ball. Three and a half turns lock-to-lock.

CHASSIS

Monocoque construction with front and rear sub-frames to carry engine, suspension etc. Sub-frames attached to body by resilient metal mountings.

1972 rubber mountings. Greasing required at steering and height control ball joints every 12,000 miles. All other joints sealed for life.

WHEELS

15 inch steel disc wheels on five studs carrying 205 x 15 radial ply tyres.

ELECTRICAL SYSTEM

12 volt alternator, with electrical operation of gear selection, front seat adjustment, windows, rear window demister (saloon), centralised door locking system, wing aerial, windscreen wipers and washers, cigar lighters front and rear, petrol filler flap, heater refrigeration and demister controls. Warning lights for hydraulic accumulator pressure, engine oil pressure, coolant level, fuel level, ignition, hand-brake/stop light bulb failure, hazard warning system.

PRINCIPAL DIMENSIONS

Overall length: 16′ 11½″
Overall height: 4′ 10¾″
Overall width: 6′ 0″
Wheelbase: 9′ 11½″
Front track: 4′ 9½″
Rear track: 4′ 9½″
Turning circle: 38′ 0″

U.K. PRICES (1973)

Rolls-Royce or Bentley Corniche Convertible   £14,203
Rolls-Royce or Bentley Corniche two-door saloon   £13,589
All coachwork by H. J. Mulliner, Park Ward Ltd.

275. The emphasis at Rolls-Royce is on craftsmanship. The men still take a great deal of pride in perfecting their work.

276. Beautifully matched picnic tables.

Painting the coachline along the side of the *Silv-*
277. *er Shadow.*

278. The final polish and the car is ready for the customer.

Index